NAVIGATING ENGLISH MEDIUM INSTRUCTION

This skills-oriented handbook for English Medium Instruction (EMI) learners provides students with a toolbox of strategies and approaches to maximise their performance in their courses.

EMI learners are students who are studying an academic subject, other than English itself, through the medium of English. Through a series of carefully designed exercises and awareness-raising tasks showcased in this book, students can develop the skills and strategies they need to optimise their academic performance in the face of considerable academic and language challenges. This accessible text is full of strategies for students to use the English language they already have in order to engage more fully in their academic courses. They will become much more efficient at preparing for, performing in, and reflecting on their classes. The book covers preparing for classes (pre-flight activities); performing in classes (in-flight strategies); and reflecting on classes (after landing).

Grounded in the research of EMI teaching and learning and in extensive teacher-training within EMI, this is a valuable resource for any EMI student studying in a university across the world, as well as EMI teachers, EAP/ESP educators, and academic support staff who work with EMI learners.

Ernesto Macaro is Emeritus Professor of Applied Linguistics at the University of Oxford. Before becoming a teacher educator and researcher in language learning he was a language teacher for 16 years. His research has focused on second language learning strategies and on the interaction between teachers and learners. He now applies these foci to classrooms where academic content is being taught through English.

Mark Searle is an Honorary Norham Fellow, Associate of the EMI Research Group and previously was a Lecturer in ELT in the University of Oxford Department of Education. For many years he was a senior consultant teacher trainer for the British Council, designing and delivering teacher training courses in EAP and EMI in universities worldwide. This experience has given him considerable insight into the needs of EMI teachers and learners in many different contexts. He has also co-designed and co-delivered EMI teacher training courses with Ernesto Macaro both in the Department of Education and abroad.

NAVIGATING ENGLISH MEDIUM INSTRUCTION

A Student Handbook

Ernesto Macaro and Mark Searle

Designed cover image: © Getty Images

First published 2025
by Routledge
605 Third Avenue, New York, NY 10158

and by Routledge
4 Park Square, Milton Park, Abingdon, Oxon, OX14 4RN

Routledge is an imprint of the Taylor & Francis Group, an informa business

© 2025 Ernesto Macaro and Mark Searle

The right of Ernesto Macaro and Mark Searle to be identified as authors of this work has been asserted in accordance with sections 77 and 78 of the Copyright, Designs and Patents Act 1988.

All rights reserved. No part of this book may be reprinted or reproduced or utilised in any form or by any electronic, mechanical, or other means, now known or hereafter invented, including photocopying and recording, or in any information storage or retrieval system, without permission in writing from the publishers.

Trademark notice: Product or corporate names may be trademarks or registered trademarks, and are used only for identification and explanation without intent to infringe.

ISBN: 978-1-032-89533-8 (hbk)
ISBN: 978-1-032-89298-6 (pbk)
ISBN: 978-1-003-54424-1 (ebk)

DOI: 10.4324/9781003544241

Typeset in Galliard
by SPi Technologies India Pvt Ltd (Straive)

CONTENTS

Some reactions of students from Sri Lanka and from Hong Kong   ix
Acknowledgments   x

CHAPTER 1
INTRODUCTORY SECTIONS   1

1.1a How to Work with This Book   3

1.1b A General Glossary of Terms Used in This Book
(How We Have Used Certain Words)   4

1.2 Your Transition from School to University   6

1.3 Let's 'Situate' Your EMI Subject   8

1.4 What Are Your EMI Lessons Like?   10

1.5 Your 'Language Support' Programme   13

1.6 Dealing with Words: Technical Words; Technical-Plus Words; General Academic Words; Everyday Words   16

CHAPTER 2
AROUND YOUR CLASSES: BEFORE TAKING OFF!   19

2.1   Strategies for You to Consider Just Before the Lesson   21

2.2   Technical and Academic Words in a Lecture   23

2.3   What Do We Mean By 'Keywords'? (Dealing With 'The Concept Iceberg')   26

2.4   Before the Lecture: Getting Ready!   30

2.5   Using the Lecture Title and Course Outline to Prepare   33

2.6   Knowing Your Lecturer's Voice and Language   35

2.7   Online Lectures and Podcasts   38

2.8   Preparing to Listen to Your Teacher: Using Audio Recordings   42

2.9   Pre-Lecture Reading: Your Own Reasons for Reading   44

2.10   Pre-Reading Around Your Classes   46

CHAPTER 3
IN-FLIGHT STRATEGIES: COPING WITH TURBULENCE   53

3.1   Note-Taking: What Goes on in Our Brains!   55

3.2   Making In-Flight Lecture Notes   57

3.3   Strategies to Think About During the Lesson   59

3.4   Discourse Markers: Navigating a Lecture   62

3.5   The Prior Knowledge Strategy When Listening   64

3.6   The IRF Sequence: What It Is For; What It Does; How to Deal with It   68

3.7	You and Your Home Language: To Use or Not to Use, that Is the Question!	74
3.8	Language Demands of Notes	76

CHAPTER 4
AROUND YOUR CLASSES: REFLECTING AFTER LANDING   81

4.1	Improving Your Note-Taking Together	83
4.2	The Power of Talking	85
4.3	Work with Coursemates: From Notes to Connected Speech	87
4.4	Accountable Talk: Making It All a Little More Formal	89
4.5	Multiword Units	92
4.6	Word Families	95
4.7	Gently Persuading Your Teachers	97
4.8	Elaborate Interrogation: How/Why?	98
4.9	Guided Reciprocal Peer Questioning: The Power of Questions and Answers!	100
4.10	Reflecting on Questions Post-Lesson	102
4.11	Examples of Socratic Questions: Invitations to Better Thinking	104
4.12	Ideas for Better Answers	107
4.13	Developing Your Range of Rhetorical Functions	109
4.14	Working on Your Own with Your Smartphone	112

4.15 Modified Cornell Notes: From In-Flight Note-Taking to
     Post-Flight Note-Making   114

4.16 Post-Class Reading for Writing   116

4.17 Writing   118

SOME REACTIONS OF STUDENTS FROM SRI LANKA AND FROM HONG KONG

"The materials are generally very useful. We wish we had learnt about this much earlier…"

"The use of the 'flight' metaphor is fun."

"…'keywords' under 'before taking off' is very reflective and thought-provoking."

"…we particularly liked the example transcripts."

"(The materials) gave me the tools I needed to participate in EMI sessions."

"(The materials) greatly improved my preparedness for college lectures."

"I haven't come across materials like this before!"

"Initiate this program throughout the world, so that students around the world could get use from these!"

ACKNOWLEDGMENTS

We would like to express our huge thanks to Daniel Fung, Jack Pun and Nadee Mahawattha for their invaluable help in trialing some of the materials contained in this book

With enormous thanks to Bev and Jules for their support and encouragement throughout

CHAPTER 1
INTRODUCTORY SECTIONS

1.1a
HOW TO WORK WITH THIS BOOK

Dear student

This book has been designed and written to help you navigate your way through the complexities of studying an academic subject through the medium of English.

The four chapters are made up of different sections that contain ideas, information and activities that you can do *before*, *during* and *after* your classes. The aim is to encourage you to develop strategies that will make learning your subject as successful as possible.

There are a number of ways that you can work with this book. You could just do the activities in the order in which they are presented. That would make sure that you are able to understand the links that we have made between the sections. However, you may not have time to do it that way or it may not suit you. In that case it is perfectly possible for you to 'dip in' to individual sections because you feel they might be useful to you. However, we would strongly encourage you to at least start with the sections contained in Chapter 1.

Whichever way you choose to work with this book, always try to write down your ideas and make notes as suggested in each section. Also, we would really encourage you to work, wherever suggested, with one or more of your classmates. You can learn so much by discussing each other's challenges and solutions.

We hope you find this book helpful, and we wish you every success with your studies.

Ernesto Macaro
and
Mark Searle

1.1b

A GENERAL GLOSSARY OF TERMS USED IN THIS BOOK (HOW WE HAVE USED CERTAIN WORDS)

EMI   English Medium Instruction (teaching a subject in English in a country that does not have English as their first language). Some people use the term 'English Medium Education' or 'Bilingual Education'.

THE SUBJECT   The academic subject you are studying through the medium of English. This is sometimes called 'the discipline' but we have used the word 'subjects'. These are subjects *other than English* itself as a subject.

GENERAL ENGLISH   The type of English you would learn in an English as a Foreign Language (EFL) class (e.g., 'how to describe your appearance').

HOME LANGUAGE   The language spoken by the majority of the population in your country. This is also sometimes called 'the first language' or 'the L1'.

ACADEMIC ENGLISH   The type of English you would use when writing an essay in your subject or the English used in the articles and books you read about in your subject, or that the teacher uses in your subject lesson.

TECHNICAL VOCABULARY   Words specific to a subject. For example: 'canine' (in dentistry), 'prevalence' (in sociology), 'abdication' (in history).

GENERAL ACADEMIC VOCABULARY   For example, 'furthermore'; 'as a result'; 'nonetheless'

EVERYDAY VOCABULARY   For example, 'let's get on with this', 'are you following me?'

LESSON   A general term for any 'class' or 'lecture'

1.2

YOUR TRANSITION FROM SCHOOL TO UNIVERSITY

Make as long a list as possible about all the similarities and differences between your last years at school and your first years at university. We have suggested one to start you off.

Aspect of my education	Similar in both school and university	Different in university from school
The number of students in the class		More students at university

When you were in your last years at school, was the subject you are now studying at university…

Taught in English?	*Taught partly in English and partly in your home language? This is sometimes referred to as 'code-mixing', 'code-switching' or 'translanguaging'*	*Taught entirely in your home language?*
Write any comments in this table		

What are the implications for you now of the transition from school to university? For example, if you were taught the subject in your home language, do you now try to remember some home language words when your teacher uses an English word? Can you think of a recent example?

_____

_____

_____

Talk to students who had a <u>different transition to you in terms of medium of instruction</u>. How did they experience that transition? Was it because of differences between school and university? Write here a few ideas that you have discovered:

_____

_____

_____

If at school you were taught your subject in the home language, were more 'technical words' (see the 'Glossary' at the beginning of this book) used than now that you are at university, or fewer technical words?

_____

_____

_____

1.3

LET'S 'SITUATE' YOUR EMI SUBJECT

Let's think about the subject(s) that you are learning through the medium of English. Would it <u>be possible</u> to learn this subject without any reference to English? Could it be taught entirely through your home language (or the L1 of the majority of the students in your classes)?

Think about some other subjects, as in the list below. In your opinion, which column do they come under? Why might this be the case? Perhaps you could do this activity with a fellow student and discuss why some subjects would be difficult to be taught without some English being used. Again, you could make some notes below the table or elsewhere.

	This subject could be taught in my home language with little or no reference to English	*It would be <u>difficult not to</u> use some English when teaching and learning this subject*
<ul><li>Anglophone literature</li><li>Applied linguistics</li><li>Architecture</li><li>Didactics of (how to teach) modern languages</li><li>Economics</li><li>Engineering</li><li>English philology (the history of words in the language)</li><li>Geography</li></ul>		

	This subject could be taught in my home language with little or no reference to English	*It would be <u>difficult not to</u> use some English when teaching and learning this subject*
• Geology • History (of your country) • International business • International relations • Internet studies • Journalism studies • Law (your country; not international) • Mathematics • Medicine • Physics • Politics • Sociology • TESOL (English Teacher Training) • Translation studies		

1.4

WHAT ARE YOUR EMI LESSONS LIKE?

Think about a typical EMI class. Which of the following best describes it:

- The teacher stands at the front, behind a desk, and talks to us about the subject. At the end of the lesson, s/he asks us if we have any questions.
- The teacher stands by the table with the computer on it and talks to us about the subject, stopping from time to time to ask us if we have understood.
- The teacher stands by the table with the computer on it but also sometimes moves around the classroom. S/he asks us questions in English, which usually require one- or two-word answers in English.
- The teacher stands by the table with the computer on it but also occasionally moves around the classroom. S/he asks us questions in English, which usually require us to reply in sentences. S/he expects us to reply in English but doesn't mind if we use our own home language.
- The teacher stands by the table with the computer on it but also moves around the classroom. S/he asks us questions in English, which usually require us to reply in sentences. S/he expects us to reply in English and will not accept answers in our own language.

o What do you think about how your teacher conducts a lesson? _____

___

o In your class, are there students with different levels of proficiency in English? If so, how does your teacher deal with these different levels?

___

o What, if anything, would you like your teacher to do differently? _____
_____

Discuss these issues with a classmate to see if they feel the same way as you do and write some notes here. _____
_____

In a typical lesson or lecture, does the teacher use slides? If s/he does, which of these scenarios best describes how the teacher uses his/her slides:

- S/he reads what is written on the slides, not much more.
- S/he reads the words/phrases that are on the slides but also talks about them at length.
- S/he reads what is on the slides but also explains what each point means by using different words. S/he 'unpacks' their meaning, like 'opening a parcel'.
- S/he rarely reads what is on the slides. The slides serve only as background information for what s/he is actually saying.

o Think about how your teacher uses slides. In what way do they help you understand the content of the lesson?
_____

o Write down what *you do* with regard to the slides.
_____

o In what way do slides help you learn new English words or bits of English language? _____

If your teacher gives you a handout with notes at the beginning of the lesson, what kind of notes are they? What do you think your teacher intends you to do with the notes?
_____

What do you do with the notes?
_____

For all the above, try to discuss your opinions with a classmate and write a few notes below.

What does EMI research suggest?
In general, research tells us that interaction between a teacher and her/his students is a good thing. Particularly, the following features of interaction are thought to be very effective for student learning:

- The teacher gives clear signals and prompts (e.g., now let's think about this…)
- A teacher asks a lot of questions as well as making lots of statements.
- The teacher asks a question, gets a response, provides feedback, then maybe asks the same student a further question, gets a slightly different response, provides some feedback and moves on.
- The teacher asks questions that are more than just checking that a student knows something…perhaps it could involve an opinion…or a more in-depth understanding of an idea.
- The teacher encourages students to use their own words and the teacher's language.
- The teacher encourages the students to respond with whole sentences or at least long phrases that contain a verb.
- The teacher provides sufficient 'wait time' (the time needed for the student to formulate an answer in their heads – see page 72) before interrupting the student or moving on to a different student.

Having completed this Introductory Section, and perhaps discussed what you had written with a classmate, what will you now do? Will you make any changes to the STRATEGIES THAT YOU USE IN CLASS? What if anything will you do differently?

_____
_____

1.5
YOUR 'LANGUAGE SUPPORT' PROGRAMME

What kind of *language support* do you get from **English Language Specialist Teachers** in your university? Write your initial thoughts in the box below.

Now compare what you have written in your box with what at least one of your classmates has written.

In most universities, English language support for EMI falls into three categories:

1. *General English* (also known as English Language Teaching): Classes focus on improving your Vocabulary and Grammar and on developing the skills of Listening, Speaking, Reading and Writing
2. *English for Academic Purposes (EAP)*: This type of course aims to develop general academic skills. It tries to address a student's needs when they are

studying a subject in any discipline. Students in an EAP classroom will probably be studying different subjects in different disciplines. However, they will all be taught about such things as 'typical academic vocabulary', 'the writer's stance', how reliable is 'the evidence that a writer presents', and also how to structure their own essays, assignments or reports.
3. *English for Specific Purposes (ESP)*: This type of course teaches students how to operate effectively 'in a particular domain' – by which is usually meant 'a specific subject or discipline'. Students will be in a classroom generally made up of students studying <u>the same or similar</u> subjects.

For you to do:

o Which body of knowledge do you think your Language Support Programme is trying to give you?
o What skills do you think your Language Support Programme is trying to give you?
o Would you like your Language Support Programme to be more specific to your EMI discipline or less specific? Why?

How does your Language Support Programme help you with understanding the content of your EMI subject/discipline?
   Does it:

ASPECTS OF YOUR LANGUAGE SUPPORT PROGRAMME	*1=YES* *2=NO* *3= A BIT*	*YOUR BRIEF COMMENT*
Deepen your understanding of your EMI subject? In what way?		
Help you to better prepare for attending lectures/classes in your EMI subject?		
Help you with reading written material in your EMI subject?		
Help you with listening to your teachers in class?		
Help you with speaking in English, for example, asking questions in class?		
Help you with making oral presentations?		
Help you with writing essays or assignments?		
Encourage you to think critically. How?		

Does the Language Support Programme have its own assessment system? If so, how does it link to the assessment in your EMI subject?

_____

_____

Now compare what you have written above with what one of your classmates has written. Are there points of disagreement? Why might this be?

_____

_____

1.6

DEALING WITH WORDS

Technical Words; Technical-Plus Words; General Academic Words; Everyday Words

You will encounter language in your classes and lectures, which comprises various categories of vocabulary. This activity is to help you think about these different categories of vocabulary.

In the table below, put a tick in the category column (or columns) that you think the word in the first column falls into.

You may have to look up some of these words on the internet. Go on! It will be worthwhile!

	Technical words (only used in one subject)	*Technical-plus words (could be used in more than one subject – or even as everyday words)*	*General academic words*	*Everyday words*
apostle				
centralisation				
code-switching				
community				
despite				
distribution				
dower				

Dealing with Words

	Technical words (only used in one subject)	Technical-plus words (could be used in more than one subject – or even as everyday words)	General academic words	Everyday words
furthermore				
lexeme				
masculinities				
military				
parasite				
proportional				
renegade				
ridiculous				
sequential				
sub-atomic				
tearful				
1				
2				
3				

You may have realised that some words fall into a number of columns. What does this mean for you as a student of your subject?

_____
_____
_____

There are three blank spaces in the above table. Can you insert three words you have recently come across in your subject and say what categories they fit into? _____

Does your teacher ever say something like: 'this is a technical word that means....'? Does the teacher then ever give you the equivalent technical word in your home language? Does this help or not help you?

_____
_____
_____

Do you ever get confused about what category a word that you read or hear falls into? If so, what do you do about it?

_____

_____

_____

Ask your teacher if you can record the first ten minutes of her/his EMI lesson. Now listen to the recording and make a list of **five new words** (ones that you have never heard before or are very unfamiliar with) that s/he used. Which of the categories above do they fall into?

_____

_____

_____

If possible, do the above activity with a fellow classmate. Did they have the same **five words**? If they did, try to discuss what category they fall into and why they are 'new' to both of you.

Were you able to work out the meaning of the words in context? Describe how you worked out a word from the context here:

_____

_____

_____

Here are some *strategies* for working out the meaning of a word:

- Looking and thinking about bits of a word that often come up. For example: '…ations' (as in 'specifications' which usually refers to nouns). 'De' in front of a word *usually* means 'no longer what follows it' as in 'demilitarized' or 'demagnetized'.
- Thinking about the phrase in which the word is located and thinking about whether your guess at the word makes sense.
- Thinking about what the word might be in your home language (L1).
- Thinking about whether the word is a technical word or not.
- Thinking about the context in which you come across the word.
- And of course….looking up the word on Google! Or in a bilingual dictionary!

Do you use any of these strategies already? Do you use any other strategies?

_____

_____

_____

CHAPTER 2
AROUND YOUR CLASSES
BEFORE TAKING OFF!

2.1
STRATEGIES FOR YOU TO CONSIDER JUST BEFORE THE LESSON

1) **Let's start with what you do as you enter your classroom…**
   What's going through your mind as you enter an EMI classroom? Do you feel anxious or confident? ….. Write down any factors that might make you feel anxious.

   _____
   _____
   _____

2) **When you enter an EMI class, is your intention to focus more on the subject you are learning or more on improving your English?**

   More on my academic subject   More on improving my English

   1 2 3 4 5 6 7 8 9 10

   Can you say why you have chosen a particular number?

   _____
   _____
   _____

   Discuss your choice with a classmate. Did they choose the same or different number? Why?

3) **Where do you sit in class?**
    At the front [ ]   at the back [ ]   at the side [ ]
    Write down any reasons why you sit where you sit.

    _____

    _____

4) **Also...who do you sit with in class?**
    Why? Here are a few ideas to help you think:
    Friends/classmates who share the same language as you?
    Students from different language and nationality backgrounds?

For each of the above questions, try to compare what you have written with what some of your classmates have written. Are you in any way surprised if their thoughts are different from yours?

2.2
TECHNICAL AND ACADEMIC WORDS IN A LECTURE

Look at the transcript from an **Economics and Business lecture**.

Don't worry if you are not familiar with some of these words. You will still be able to do the task.

THE OBJECTIVE OF THIS TASK IS TO HELP YOU BETTER UNDERSTAND THE DIFFERENT TYPES OF WORDS IN A LECTURE

Even if this is not your subject, try to identify which words you think are....

Technical words (only used in this subject)
Academic words (could be used in a number of different subjects)
Everyday words (you might hear them in a London street or a New York bar). ☺

TEACHER: fair value right? a revaluation if you adopt the revaluation model of course it is allowed if you if you adopt the cost model it is not allowed er is a subsequent measurement of an asset as its er its fair value which is the er hypothetical price that you er erm of a hypothetical transaction in an active market ok for that specific asset. this is, that was a tricky part the revaluation gains, what are they?, er what what is it revaluation gain? ....

It's a I mean you put it in a reserve, it's, ok if you have a carrying value in your balance sheet the netbook value and you make a revaluation at fair value you have a gain if that is higher ok? if you increase the value of your asset, meaning

	that fair value is, higher er than the cost than the than the er the netbook value the carry value that you had, and is a kind of income not realized meaning that you didn't receive it's not a t a real tr… it's not a transaction but is an increase in value in your asset that determines also an increase in the equities side in order to have the balance sheet that balances if you increase the value of the assets you also have to increase something on the on the other side and that something is in the equities side. So how are they treated in the balance sheet? I've just just told you actually, where do you show the revaluation gains in the balance sheet?…in the in the within the equities as a reserve, and that reserve cannot be distributed cannot be given to shareholders ok? If you adopt the revaluation model, the principle is the same, but on the left side within the asset you don't have the cost but you have the f…..
STUDENT:	fair value
TEACHER:	fair value, so the net the carrying value of er assets that are measured with the revaluation method is fair value less accumulated depreciation less accumulated impairment these things are, well you will have it also with the with the slides er it's a kind of summary if you want then, of course you maybe you should go if you don't remember what is a recoverable amount how some get computed you go back to the book and you look at it but these are important ok these things to evaluate assets, are you ok with this?

Was it easy to categorise the words in this lecture? WHAT STRATEGIES MIGHT YOU USE IN YOUR OWN LECTURES TO IDENTIFY THE DIFFERENT CATEGORIES AND DEAL WITH THEM IF NECESSARY?

Even if this is not your subject…which words would you have wanted this teacher to explain further? Why those particular words? Was it because:

- You had never come across the word before?
- The word is a concept and needs lots of other words to explain it.

Now try to record 15 minutes of one of your lessons and transcribe it in the way we have done above. You might want to do this with a classmate – that is, you both independently transcribe the 15 minutes and then compare.

Once again, put the words into categories of: technical; general academic; everyday language.

Technical and Academic Words in a Lecture 25

Word or phrase	technical	general academic	everyday language

Now let's think about the language that your teacher used in those 15 minutes of his/her lecture. Did they:

- Use any codeswitching (L1 use)? If so, write down a few words they 'switched'
- If so, why did they switch to your (or other students') L1?
- Did it help you to understand the meaning of the word if they 'switched'? How did it help?
- Did switching, do you think, pose any problems for other students in the class?

Write down some of your answers here and perhaps compare them with a classmate.

_____
_____
_____
_____

2.3

WHAT DO WE MEAN BY 'KEYWORDS'? (DEALING WITH 'THE CONCEPT ICEBERG')

> **GLOSSARY**
>
> *encapsulate*   to express succinctly the essential features of something

> **NOTE**
>
> In the picture of the iceberg below, we are using a 'technical term' to refer to a 'label' that is applied to difficult ideas and concepts.

Whenever we do research with EMI students, they often tell us that they have problems with the 'keywords' in a lecture or lesson. But what do they mean by the 'keywords'?

Think about what <u>you</u> mean by this or, better still, try to discuss what keywords are with a classmate. Here are some possibilities. What do you think?

- Keywords in a lesson are the ones that the teacher says we should make a note of and/or remember.
- Keywords in a lesson are the ones that the teacher uses over and over again.
- Keywords in a lesson are the technical words the teacher uses (either verbally or on slides etc.).

What Do We Mean By 'Keywords'?   **27**

- Keywords in a lesson are the 'labels' given to difficult ideas and concepts.
- Keywords in a lesson are the ones I decide I need to remember for future use.

The 'Concept Iceberg'

'Homeomorphism' is a technical term (or label) given to a 'concept' in mathematics. If you are not studying mathematics don't worry if you don't understand it! However, do take a good look at our picture of 'the iceberg'. The definition of the concept is:

> *In the mathematical field of topology, a homeomorphism or topological isomorphism or bi-continuous function is a continuous function between topological spaces that has a continuous inverse function.*

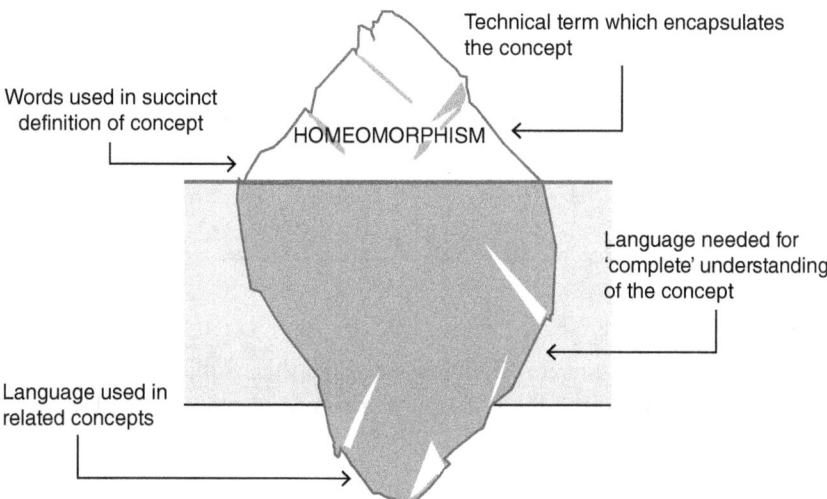

So, what might cause students difficulty when they tell us they have difficulty with 'keywords'? Is it the 'label' (the words used to define the concept) or the language needed to fully understand it?

> Now think of a 'label' given to a difficult idea or concept in your subject and write it here:
>
> ....
>
> Now try to find (or remember) a definition of that idea or concept that you have been given by your teacher or have read in a textbook (or online etc.) and write it here:

> What do you find most challenging to remember?
>
> The label itself? Why?
>
> The definition? If so, why?
>
> Some of the individual words used in the definition? If so, why?

Keyword Practice

A very useful resource for students studying their subject through the medium of English is the BASE corpus (British Academic Spoken English), which has been compiled by the University of Warwick: https://www.coventry.ac.uk/research/research-directories/current-projects/2015/british-academic-spoken-english-corpus-base/

Go to the corpus and try to find a lecture that is associated with the subject you are studying. It doesn't have to be exactly the same subject but one that you are at least 'broadly familiar' with. Ideally, you might do this with a fellow student in your class.

Go to a section where the teacher is using a lot of 'keywords' or 'concept labels'
What might you have difficulty with in this particular text:
The label itself? Why?

The definition? If so, why?

Some of the individual words used in the definition? If so, why?

If you have done this activity with a classmate in your own subject, did you have the same ideas about this problem of 'keywords'?

2.4
BEFORE THE LECTURE
Getting Ready!

WHAT EMI STUDENTS SAY

I listen to podcasts, documentaries and short readings.
I study the contents of each session.
In case there were specialised terms for the course, then I would read a text in English.
Normally, I re-read my notes.

GLOSSARY

to participate in	to play an active part in
to anticipate	to expect or predict
criticality	the ability to question or evaluate what you hear, read or learn
academic thinking	the logical processes, use of evidence and criticality used in your discipline to solve problems, discuss issues or create disciplinary knowledge
prior knowledge	what you already know about a subject
verbal	expressed in words, usually spoken
transitions	changes from one section to another

Many EMI students do not prepare for lectures in English – or, if they do some preparation, usually do the same things they do for lectures in their first language. This is not necessarily good preparation – as participating in a lecture in English is very different to participating in your first language.

So, it is important to prepare for a lecture in English!

Your preparation should focus on:

o Your understanding of the purpose of the lecture
o How you anticipate the structure and organisation of the lecture
o What you do or don't know about the content of the lecture
o How you anticipate the language/vocabulary challenges of the lecture.

The Purpose of the Lecture

Understanding the purpose of a lecture will directly affect what you do before, during and after it.

Can you complete the following sentences?

o This lecture is important because …
o In this lecture, I expect to learn …
o This lecture will help me in my examinations because …
o Before this lecture I will …
o During this lecture I will …
o After this lecture I will …

If possible, discuss your answers with some classmates. If you have different answers, try to find out why you think differently.

Now focus on these questions:

o What about the content of the lecture? Do you need to understand and remember everything? If so, how does this affect what you do in the lecture?
o How does the lecture content relate to your examinations and how you are assessed? Do you need to remember and repeat the content? Or do you need to demonstrate academic thinking and criticality?
o In addition to informational content, does your lecturer demonstrate academic thinking, problem solving and criticality? If so, how do you record this for learning purposes?
o Are the lectures on this course different/similar to your experience at high school or a previous university?

The Structure and Organisation of the Lecture

How you anticipate the structure and organisation of the lecture affects how well you can navigate your way through the content and details.

Think about these things:

- Is there a normal structure to your lectures?
    - Which of these sections do you anticipate your lecture having?
        - Welcome/Administration and reminders
        - Review of previous lecture(s)
        - Introduction to the current lecture
        - Main points
        - Conclusion
- How does your lecturer signal the transitions from one part of a lecture to the next?
    - Is this verbal? Does the lecturer tell you when transitions are happening?
        - What key words or phrases are used to indicate transitions? Make a brief list of possible phrases below:

        _____
        _____
        _____
        _____

    - Is this visual? Does the lecturer indicate transitions with new PowerPoint slides?

Prior Knowledge

- What is the focus or subject of the lecture?
- Does the lecture have a title? What are the key words in the title?
- Is there any pre-reading you need to do?
- Is the lecture part of a sequence of lectures?
- If so, how does this lecture fit into the sequence?
- What lectures have gone before this one?
- What knowledge would be helpful to bring to this lecture?
- Is there any technical vocabulary or language you expect to hear in this lecture?

2.5
USING THE LECTURE TITLE AND COURSE OUTLINE TO PREPARE

GLOSSARY

course outline   the description of the course provided by your university
paraphrase   to put into other words, often for the purpose of clarity or simplification
clarity   clearness, easy to understand
simplification   made simple with difficulties removed
prior knowledge   what you already know about a subject

The title of the lecture is a very useful resource when preparing to listen. Think about it carefully. Use this with the course outline to direct your thinking.

o What are the key words in the title?
o Are there any technical words? How familiar are you with the concepts related to the technical words?
o Can you paraphrase the title using different words?
o Can you translate the title into your first language?
o How familiar are you with the subject and its English language?
o If you know nothing or very little about the subject of the lecture, what will you do to improve this before the lecture?

o What do you already know about this subject? Make some brief notes to summarise your knowledge. Use the course outline to direct you. Use spider-grams or mind-maps.
o What content/language do you expect to hear in the lecture?
o What about the technical vocabulary related to this lecture? What technical words do you already know? Make a spider-gram of related vocabulary. Review your vocabulary cards.
o What non-technical vocabulary do you expect to hear? This is a difficult question, but an important one!
o If you have the opportunity, speak to some classmates about your pre-lecture thinking. Do your classmates have any thoughts that are different from yours?

Complete a K-W-L table to help activate your prior knowledge.

What do I already KNOW?	*What do I WANT to learn?*	*What did I LEARN?*

Making your own anticipation guide
   Create a list of:

- Five key questions you expect to be answered in the lecture.
- List any areas of difficulty you expect during the lecture.
- What new things do you expect to learn?

Use your anticipation guide to discuss the lecture with classmates.

2.6
KNOWING YOUR LECTURER'S VOICE AND LANGUAGE

WHAT EMI STUDENTS SAY

On certain occasions, a lecturer will have a very heavy accent (be it regional or from abroad), which can be quite distracting. In particularly undesirable cases, the lecturer will sometimes even mispronounce terms.

Since our quantum mechanics professor is German, English is not his native tongue, so sometimes it was a little bit difficult to follow what he was saying.

Yes. There have been times when the teacher has a lot of accent, and when English was spoken, there would be words or phrases that were strange to be understood.

GLOSSARY

distracting	takes your attention away from the thing you should be concentrating on
opaque	not clear, difficult to understand
code	a system of communication using symbols and/or numbers.
hesitate	to pause during speech in order to think

DOI: 10.4324/9781003544241-15

reduced forms	shorter forms of words (often informal) eg. *gonna* for going to; *rock'n'roll* for rock and roll
idioms	phrases that are not easily understood by decoding the meaning of the individual words in them. For example, I can't see the woods for the trees; I can't make head nor tail of this! Some idioms may be more or less opaque than others.
colloquial language	informal language often found in friendly social contexts
intonation	rise, fall, rhythm and stress patterns in speech to support meaning
monotone	flat, with no ups or downs

In any listening situation, including lectures, your ability to make sense of what is said begins with the voice and language of the speaker. Think of the English language as a *code* delivered by your lecturer and think of your job as *decoding*. To understand this code, you will need to understand the sounds your lecturer makes as well as the words s/he uses.

- **Task**: Think about your lecturer's voice and speaking style. Use these ideas below to guide your thinking:
  o **Accent**: does your lecturer have an accent? Does this present any problem to you?
  o **Speed of talking**: how quickly does your lecturer talk? Can you follow?
  o **Pauses**: does your lecturer pause often enough to allow you to think?
  o **Hesitations**: does your lecturer hesitate a lot? Does this cause you any difficulty?
  o **Clarity of pronunciation**: do you find it easy to understand your lecturer?
  o **Volume**: does your lecturer speak quietly or with good volume?
  o **Reduced forms**: does your lecturer use any reduced or informal language?
  o **Idioms/colloquial language**: does your lecturer use idiomatic phrases or expressions that you find difficult to understand?
  o **Cultural references**: does your lecturer make any cultural references that you do not understand?

- o **Vocabulary**: does your lecturer use lots of words you do not really understand?
- o **Sentences**: does your lecturer use short or long, complicated sentences?
- o **Intonation**: does your lecturer have a flat, monotone voice – or does s/he use stress and rise and fall patterns to emphasise meaning
- **Task**: What can you do to better decode your lecturer's voice and language? Note some thoughts below:

_____
_____
_____
_____

2.7
ONLINE LECTURES AND PODCASTS

WHAT EMI STUDENTS SAY

Online lectures are a great resource whenever in-person lectures don't quite cut it.

I use online lectures that the professors recommend to us.

Yes. When I'm interested in a subject, I look for them online and since there is more material in English, then I can complement the things I saw in class.

GLOSSARY

complement	improve the quality
invaluable	extremely important
optimise your ability	to improve to the best of your ability
visual cue	something you can see that tells you something predictable is about to happen
gestures	hand movement with specific meanings e.g. thumbs up
posture	the way you stand or hold your body

DOI: 10.4324/9781003544241-16

to tune in to their voice	to become familiar with the characteristics of your lecturer's voice
synchronicity	things happening at the same time
lip-sync	to synchronise your lip movements with the speech of someone else.
repertoire	the list of skills, techniques or performances available to an individual.

Many universities provide online recordings of lectures – these may be video or audio recordings. For an EMI student, these are invaluable resources that may help you to develop lecturer-specific listening/decoding skills. Every lecturer presents you with different listening challenges depending on the voice and language characteristics considered in the previous section.

Your ability to decode each lecturer can be improved by preparing and practising. Try some of the techniques below.

Preparing to Listen to Your Lecturer – Using Video Lectures

The following are Pre-lecture techniques to optimise your ability to decode your lecturer's voice through visual cues and clues.

- **Looking Helps Listening**
    o Play the video recording with the sound ON
    o Focus on your lecturer's lip movements and facial expressions
    o Look out for hand movements and gestures – does your lecturer have a repertoire of hand movements and gestures for particular purposes?
    o Body language and posture can also help you decode the lecture.
- **Silent Listening**
    o Play the video recording with the sound OFF
    o Use as many of the visual clues as you can to work out what your lecturer might be saying! (Difficult but very useful!)
- **Lip-Sync the Lecturer!**
    o Watch a short section of the lecture several times with the sound ON.
    o Make a few notes if you wish.
    o Now play the section again with the sound OFF.
    o You are now the lecturer! Can you lip-sync the lecturer's words – or your version of them! Do this silently and then with words!!
    o Do you notice any language problems? Make a note of them!

- **Mirror the screen!**
    - o Choose a short, two-minute section of the video.
    - o Pay careful attention to the body language and gestures used by the lecturer.
    - o Watch two or three times.
    - o Play the section again; this time try to mirror your lecturers hand movements and gestures. Try to copy in real time, synchronising your movements with those on the screen!
- **You are the Lecturer!**
    - o Having tried some of the above techniques, try to deliver a section of the lecture on your own!
    - o How successful were you?
    - o Make a note of any difficulties and decide what you need to do about them!

An Important Note on PowerPoint

How does your lecturer interact with PowerPoint or any other visual aids? Getting familiar with your lecturer's use of visual information to supplement the spoken lecture is highly beneficial. Consider these points:

- o Synchronicity: Does your lecturer synchronise talk and screen?
- o Time to read: Does your lecturer give you time to read and understand a new slide before talking over/through it? Most people will prioritise reading over listening, and they are unable to listen and read effectively at the same time. How could you manage this?
- o Less is more: Does your lecturer put too much information on slides?

An Important Note on Cultural Differences

Different cultures may use different gestures and have different *vocabularies* for their body language. If you and your lecturer come from different cultures, can you notice any differences in your non-verbal communication? How would you develop your understanding and ability to recognise these differences?

An Important Note About Finding Lectures Online

Finding lectures online to complement your studies can be very beneficial – but you need to be careful! Here are some considerations:

- o Where was the lecture recorded?
- o Why was the lecture recorded?

o When was the lecture recorded?
o Is the subject of the lecture relevant to your course?

As a rule, podcasts provided by other universities can be very helpful – as long as the subject matter is up-to-date and relevant University of Oxford Podcasts (2024). Be more careful of other sources of videos! The safest option is only to use online lectures recommended by your lecturers!

A very useful resource for online lectures is The University of Oxford Podcasts site: https://podcasts.ox.ac.uk

Spend some time getting familiar with the site and the resources that might help you.

References

Oxford University podcasts (2024) Available at: https://podcasts.ox.ac.uk (Accessed 15 July 2024)

2.8

PREPARING TO LISTEN TO YOUR TEACHER

Using Audio Recordings

> **GLOSSARY**
>
> *time on task*   time spent doing a job or piece of work
> *gesture*   a movement, usually of the hand to indicate or support a particular meaning or message
> *transitioning* moving or changing from one thing to another

Below are some techniques and approaches you can use to optimise your ability to decode your lecturer's voice through audio cues and clues. Audio recordings are more challenging than video recordings but can be very helpful. (Note: Some of these techniques can also be applied to video recordings)

- **Time on Task**
    - The more often we do something, the better chance we have of improving!
    - Download an audio recording to a device.
    - Consider listening while walking to class, shopping or on the bus.
- **Pause and Rewind**
    - Don't be afraid to pause and rewind when you don't quite catch something!
    - Re-listen until you get a better understanding.
    - If you don't get it – make a note and ask a classmate if they can decode the words!

DOI: 10.4324/9781003544241-17

- **Listen, Repeat, Repeat**
  - Choose a 5-second section of the recording
  - Listen very carefully
  - Pause the recording and try to repeat the lecturer's words?
  - Repeat as necessary
  - If you are feeling confident, try this with a 10-second section
- **Listen, Repeat and Count**
  - Work with one or two classmates
  - As above, choose a short 10-second section of the recording
  - Listen very carefully and count the number of words used by the lecturer
  - Compare your answers
  - Listen again until you agree on the same number!
- **Listen, Repeat and Summarise**
  - Work alone or with a classmate
  - Choose a 5-minute section of the lecture
  - Listen twice
  - Make your own written or spoken summary of the section
  - Compare and evaluate each other's summary
- **Technical Vocabulary Checklists**
  - Choose a 10-minute section of the lecture
  - Listen carefully and write down all the technical vocabulary used by the lecturer
  - Listen again and check. Use the pause button if necessary
- **Transitions and Changes**
  - Transitions and changes. In any lecture, it is important to recognise when your lecturer is transitioning to a new point/subject or is changing focus. Use your audio recording to focus on any linguistic strategies they use so you can better recognise them in live lectures. Notice how your lecturer signals transitions with words/phrases, and changes of voice.

Using audio podcasts can be very helpful in practising these skills: https://podcasts.ox.ac.uk

Access this website and navigate to audio recordings of relevant lectures University of Oxford Podcasts (2024).

References

Oxford University podcasts (2024) Available at: https://podcasts.ox.ac.uk (Accessed 15 July 2024).

2.9

PRE-LECTURE READING

Your Own Reasons For Reading

> **WHAT EMI STUDENTS SAY**
>
> I normally do the readings prior to the class and I re-read my notes.
> I prepare for them in the same manner as my other courses, usually with some prior reading.

> **GLOSSARY**
>
> *relevant* — connected or appropriate to what is being considered, discussed or done
>
> *disciplinary thinking skills* — the type of thinking needed in your academic subject including criticality, judgement and knowledge building

Lecturers often give you pre-lecture reading. Think carefully about this pre-reading.

> **Task:** make a note of three reasons for pre-reading for lectures
> 1.
> 2.
> 3.

Now look at these generally accepted reasons for academic pre-reading:

- Pre-reading for lectures helps you to…
    o develop and build relevant subject knowledge.
    o develop relevant subject vocabulary.
    o develop your disciplinary thinking skills and criticality.
    o become a more engaged and thoughtful listener/participant in lectures
    o optimise the benefit of attending the lecture(s)
- Task: think carefully about the above reasons and how they might influence your approach to pre-reading texts. How, for example, would the reasons above influence how you take notes?

_____
_____
_____
_____

- Can you think of any other reasons?

2.10
PRE-READING AROUND YOUR CLASSES

> **WHAT EMI STUDENTS SAY**
>
> ... sometimes I don't understand some technical words or some context of the words.
> Even in Spanish I have difficulties!
> Sometimes I get stuck with specific words.
> Once I had to read 500 pages in 2 days, and I was not even prepared to read that amount of pages, so I struggled a lot!

> **GLOSSARY**
>
> *prescribed reading list*   a reading list given to you by your lecturer
> *to prioritise*   to recognise as important and possibly do first
> *optimise*   to make as good as possible
> *determined by*   caused, made to happen

It is important to think carefully about the nature of pre-reading and its purposes. In the previous section, we considered this list of reasons:

- develop and build relevant subject knowledge.
- develop relevant subject vocabulary.

- develop your disciplinary thinking skills and criticality.
- become a more engaged and thoughtful listener/participant in lectures
- optimise the benefit of attending the lecture(s)

We will now think about each one of these in more detail.

Relevant Subject Knowledge

The key word here is *relevant*. In your context, this is probably determined by two key factors:

- Your prescribed reading lists
- The title of the upcoming lecture or class.

Prescribed Reading Lists

It is important that you understand the difference between *essential reading* – that is, the reading you must do before a class and *additional reading* – that is, non-essential reading that may be completed before or after a class. If you are not sure about this, ask your lecturer. If your lecturer is not available, discuss this with some classmates.

You must prioritise essential reading and make sure you do not schedule it for the last minute. Remember that reading in English is usually slower than reading in your first language, so you will need more time. As a general rule, give yourself between 30% and 50% more time for shorter texts and up to 100% more for longer, more difficult texts.

It is very likely that your essential pre-reading texts will form the prior knowledge that you need to take to your classes – in other words, the relevant subject knowledge will be contained in these texts. It is essential, therefore, that you work hard on these texts to develop both your subject knowledge and the language required to express it.

Relevant Subject Vocabulary

As described earlier in this section, vocabulary works like an iceberg. It is important that you remember this and do not just focus on the technical vocabulary of the subject – above the surface. Remember the vocabulary under the water!

Vocabulary Cards

It is a very good idea to make vocabulary learning part of your (pre-)reading routine. A very quick and effective way to collect and remember new words or phrases is to make small vocabulary cards – you can use paper if you wish. The cards should be about this size:

On one side of the card, write the new word. On the other side, you have a few options.

o You could write a simple definition in English
o You could write a definition in your first language
o You could write one or two sentences including the new word
o You could write a translation
o You could use a symbol or icon instead of words to help you remember the meaning of the new word

To help you remember, you could be creative and use different colours, fonts and upper/lower case letters!

How to use your Vocabulary Cards:

o Collect cards into groups of up to about 50 – smaller groups are of course possible!
o Keep the cards together with a rubber band.
o Keep the cards in your bag or pocket.
o When you have some down time – for example, on the bus or walking home – take the cards out and test yourself.
o If possible, work with a friend and test each other.
o Lay ten of the cards down on your desk face up. Study them for 2 minutes, then remove them from sight. How many of the words can you remember? You could do the same thing with the cards the other way up.
o As you collect different groups of words, occasionally mix them up to give you some random practice!
o Try to look at your cards as often as you can – and certainly just before classes.

Online Resources to Help Develop Your Vocabulary

There are many online resources available for developing your non-technical vocabulary, and you may already be using some. Oxford University Press has developed some really helpful wordlists to help you check and develop your vocabulary for both academic and non-academic words and phrases: https://www.oxfordlearnersdictionaries.com/wordlists/

Moving from the Oxford 3,000 to the Oxford 5,000

These are *underwater words* and are the essential base for your English language: https://www.oxfordlearnersdictionaries.com/wordlists/oxford3000-5000

The Oxford 3,000 is a list of high-frequency vocabulary that every learner needs to know. The list is organised into proficiency levels (CEFR A1 – B2 i.e., beginner to intermediate). You need to check that you know all of these words.

o Look at the words in each level and check you know them.
o For any new words – make a vocabulary card!

When you have checked all of the 3,000 words move on to the Oxford 5,000. This longer list contains an additional 2,000 words at an advanced level (CEFR B2 – C2). Ideally, you need to know all of these words too! Don't try to learn all these in one day – focus on:

o Using the lists to identify the words you do not yet know
o Using the word lists to learn 10–20 words a day
o Use the word lists to search for new non-technical words you discover in your reading.

Developing Your Academic Vocabulary

The OPAL is a checklist of academic words and phrases, organised by level, that you need for academic speaking and writing Oxford Learners Dictionaries (2024): https://www.oxfordlearnersdictionaries.com/wordlists/opal

Ideally, you will know all of these words and phrases – so you need to check which of the words and phrases you do and don't yet know. When you have done this, start making vocabulary cards for the words and phrases that are new to you.

Making and using vocabulary cards is a good start for developing your vocabulary but you also need to:

o Notice these new words and phrases when you read or hear them. Each time you meet a new word your understanding and memory develop, so make a conscious effort to notice these words when reading texts and lectures.
o Use these new words and phrases in writing and speaking when possible. Remember – use them or lose them!

Develop Your Reading Speed

You will probably read more slowly in English than in your first language. You can, however, improve your reading fluency in English. This requires deliberate, repeated practice – a little and often. Some key points for you:

o Be a reader – read often!
o Read outside of your academic course. Find things that interest you and read!
o Remember to read easy texts – not just difficult academic texts.
o Work out – on average – how many words you can read a minute in English. Find five or six academic texts. Copy and paste them into Word or similar. Read for a minute. Stop and use Word Count to track your speed. Average this over five or six texts.
o Aim to improve your speed by 10–15% in the first instance.
o When reading, occasionally speed up by 10–15% for a paragraph or two. Stop and check how much you remember!
o Try not to *finger read* that is, do not trace your finger along the line!
o Try to focus on two points of each line: the first approximately one third from the left side of the page; the second approximately two thirds from the left side of the page. Use these points to try and see the words before and after them.

Develop Your Academic Thinking Skills and Criticality

When pre-reading it is important to be an active reader! As an EMI university student, you are not a *passive receiver* of information. You are an *active constructor* of your own knowledge and language. Reading is essential to this process. Reading is a thinking activity.

- **Task**: think carefully. How can you read a pre-reading text as an active constructor of your knowledge and language? List some ideas below:
  _____
  _____
  _____

Some ideas for reading as an active constructor!

o Always look out for what is new in both knowledge and language.
o Highlight new things!
o Read with questions in mind. Think about how and why as you read.
o What is the key evidence? What are the key findings? Are these credible?
o Constructors connect! As you read, try to connect what you are reading to what you already know. Use old knowledge to help you with the new stuff!
o Stop and think! Take time to stop and think about what you are reading.
o Think about the class or lecture you are pre-reading for. What parts of your reading are especially relevant?

Become a More Engaged and Thoughtful Listener/Participant in Lectures

Just as you are an active constructor when you read, you are also an active constructor in lectures. Listening is not a passive activity – it is an active interrogation of what you hear!

Pack Your Bags and Enjoy the Journey

Pre-reading is a way of *packing your bags* in preparation for a class. The better your packing, the better your experience of the class! Think about it – knowledge attracts knowledge. If you have done your pre-reading effectively, you will be ready to use this *prior knowledge* to learn effectively.

o Try to connect what you hear to your pre-reading.
o Does this support your pre-reading or is it different?
o What ideas in your pre-reading can you hear in the class?
o Does your lecturer use any of the technical vocabulary you first met in your pre-reading?

Thinking about the above points will help make the lecture more interesting for you and keep you focused.

Optimise the Benefit of Attending the Lecture

Imagine the difference between attending a lecture having done no pre-reading and attending a lecture having completed all your pre-reading. You will agree that the second option is by far the best.

It is possible that you might not understand everything in a lecture, especially if the content is new. Pre-reading gives you a much better chance! Pre-reading gives you:

o content
o language
o ideas
o understanding

All of these will optimise your performance in the lecture!

References

Oxford Learners' Dictionaries Wordlists (2024) Available at: https://www.oxfordlearnersdictionaries.com/wordlists/ (Accessed: 16 July 2024)

CHAPTER 3
IN-FLIGHT STRATEGIES
COPING WITH TURBULENCE

3.1

NOTE-TAKING

What Goes on in Our Brains!

GLOSSARY

economical saves time, saves effort.
convert change from one form to another
monitor keep thinking about

How do you take notes during a lesson? Think carefully, and then make a list here of how you go about taking notes:

_____
_____

Now discuss this with a fellow student and find out if their method of taking notes is different from yours, and write some differences here:

_____
_____

Some Theories Behind Note-Taking

When the human brain listens to speech, it tends to convert language into ideas, concepts or even images that represent those ideas and concepts. It does this because it is more 'economical' to store an idea in your brain than to store vast quantities of language that someone has said to you. Just think of something interesting that you have read on the internet recently. Do you remember the ideas in the text or the actual words?

Of course there are occasions when what you want to do is remember the exact words someone said to you so that you can then tell someone else… something like: 'Do you know what she said to me….????', 'You'll never guess!!!!' But this doesn't happen very often.

When we take notes of what we are listening to in a lesson (we might also call this 'summarising'), we also (usually!) try to convert language into ideas because, as we have said, it is more economical for the brain to store ideas, facts and concepts than the actual language used. So then the question is, how should you take notes? Should you always use your own words rather than the teacher's words? In some ways that would be ideal because it would ensure that an attempt has been made by you to properly understand the concept. However, if you do this, then you need to make more decisions:

- Should I use my own words in English?
- Should I use my own words but in my home language?
- Should I use my own words but use a mixture of both languages?

Sometimes you just have to use the actual language you have heard because you decide that's the best way of expressing something. So this is a tricky problem and it is difficult to give confident advice about this. Probably the best advice is:

- Try different methods
- Monitor and evaluate which one is working best for you
- Discuss with other students how they take notes

Fundamentally though what you are doing is:

- Stage 1: Listening to language
- Stage 2: Converting bits of language into ideas/concepts
- Stage 3: Converting the ideas back into language (whether it is all your own language, or some of the teacher's, will depend on the type of concept)

Stages two and three are the crucial stages in note-taking. Stage two requires accurate understanding of the language's meaning.

3.2
MAKING IN-FLIGHT LECTURE NOTES

WHAT EMI STUDENTS SAY

Lots of them (notes) so that I can remember and practice new words or concepts (if given).

I write the main ideas always in original language of the lecture and using symbols or drawings

I have a notebook where I write the concepts, brief definitions and key words. I like to use more than 2 different colours so that I can remember concepts better.

GLOSSARY

in-flight lecture notes	notes taken by a student <u>during</u> a lecture
academic discipline	your academic subject or academic course (e.g., architecture)
assessed paper	written course work that is examined and graded
a preliminary draft	a first version or first attempt at writing
transformative	changing from one thing into another

Why Take Notes?

Task: look at these ten possible reasons for taking notes during a lecture. Which are most relevant to you?

Taking notes in lectures...

1. Helps me to focus and concentrate.
2. Helps me to better understand the content.
3. Shows me if I do not fully understand something.
4. Helps to immerse me in the language of the subject.
5. Helps me to remember the content.
6. Helps me to think and develop my criticality.
7. Gives me a starting point for written assignments.
8. Helps to develop my writing fluency in English.
9. Gives me a document to compare with classmates.
10. Helps me to prepare for examinations.

Notes as a First Step in a Transformative Process

Making notes in English, from an English-medium lecture, presents some additional reasons for note-taking. Essentially, you are doing the same as in your first language but with the added consideration of the English language – or more specifically the English language required within your academic discipline. This is very important indeed, so it is useful to think about the act of in-flight note-taking as both a content and language exercise.

You may be required to submit assessed papers or have to take written examinations in English. If so, your grade will not just depend on what you know – it will depend on what you are able to communicate in English.

With these objectives or obligations in mind, making notes in English can also be seen as the first step in a transformative process – a process in which you take the language and content of the lecture and transform it into something else. This could be an essay, a paper or perhaps a spoken presentation. As the first step, your in-flight notes do not need to be perfect – they are very much a preliminary draft for you to develop and improve after the lecture.

We will look at this post-lecture development process later, but for now, let's look at what you can do to get ready for a lecture in English.

3.3
STRATEGIES TO THINK ABOUT DURING THE LESSON

Let's think about what you personally do <u>during the class or lecture</u>. Let's think about it particularly in connection with *understanding vocabulary*. For each of the following say whether what you do is 'very much like me' 'not at all like me' or somewhere in between. You could agree to do this separately with a classmate and then compare notes.

I try to identify the keywords in a lesson	**Very much like me**.........................**Not at all like me**
I write down the words the teacher says are important	**Very much like me**.........................**Not at all like me**
I try to make connections in my head between what is written on slides/whiteboard and what the teacher is saying	**Very much like me**.........................**Not at all like me**
I try to make notes of the explanations the teacher gives me in English	**Very much like me**.........................**Not at all like me**
I try to make notes of the explanations the teacher gives me in my own language	**Very much like me**.........................**Not at all like me**

DOI: 10.4324/9781003544241-23

I am aware or the different types of vocabulary I hear (every day vocabulary; general academic vocabulary; technical vocabulary)	Very much like me.........................Not at all like me
I try to work out the meaning of an English word I don't know from the sentence that it appears in	Very much like me.........................Not at all like me
I try to work out the meaning of an English word I don't know by looking it up on my device	Very much like me.........................Not at all like me
I put my hand up and ask the teacher to explain technical words or phrases in English;	Very much like me.........................Not at all like me
I make a list of words that are new to me, and that the teacher does not explain	Very much like me.........................Not at all like me
I make a list of words which look the same in English as in my home language	Very much like me.........................Not at all like me
I try to see if the beginnings or the ends of words give me a clue as to their meaning	Very much like me......................... Not at all like me
I ask the person next to me for an explanation of a word I don't know	Very much like me.........................Not at all like me
When I haven't understood a whole concept/idea/theory I ask the teacher to explain it again in English;	Very much like me.........................Not at all like me

| When I haven't understood a whole concept/idea/theory I ask the teacher to explain it again in my home language | **Very much like me**........................**Not at all like me** |

On a scale from 1 (min.) to 10 (max), what proportion of the notes you make in class are in English?

                10 9 8 7 6 5 4 3 2 1

What do you think are the benefits of making notes in English?
_____
_____
_____

What do you think are the benefits of making notes in your home language?
_____
_____
_____

Now compare once again your notes with a those of a classmate.

3.4

DISCOURSE MARKERS

Navigating a Lecture

What Are They and What Are They Used For?

Discourse markers are the words or short phrases that link bits of speech or indicate something that the hearer (the person who is listening to the speaker) should take special note of. They should help you to find your way (navigate) through a lecture.

Some of these we are sure you are already very familiar with:

Consequently,
and therefore,
As a result.

Others are often used specifically in classes and lectures to shift the focus of attention:

Now let's have a look at…
OK, moving on from…
right, having established that…

There are many useful academic resources online for students who want to improve their listening skills in English. For example, you could try the University of Oxford Podcasts, which are available either in audio or video: https://staged.podcasts.ox.ac.uk/

Go to the website and try to find a lecture or podcast that is associated with the subject you are studying. It doesn't have to be exactly the same subject but one that you are at least 'broadly familiar' with. You may find it useful to do this with a classmate.

In the lecture, try to identify the discourse markers that the presenter is using.

How does s/he use them? _____
_____

Are they used frequently? _____
_____

What do you think the presenter is trying to do when s/he uses them?
_____
_____

Do you think the use of these discourse markers is helpful? Why?
_____
_____
_____

- Now ask your teacher if you can audio record some or all of one of his/her lessons. Then listen to the recording and see if you can spot some of the discourse markers.
- Think back to the lesson itself and how these affected you as you were listening. Do you remember what you did at the time? As always, try to discuss these issues with a classmate.

3.5

THE PRIOR KNOWLEDGE STRATEGY WHEN LISTENING

> **GLOSSARY**
>
> *diverges from*   moves away from; is different from
> *conjures up*   brings up in your mind

You will have already used this strategy when you were learning English *as a subject* (General English Class). For example, the teacher may have asked you to listen to a text about a holiday. As soon as you knew that it was about a holiday, it should have activated (made connections with) in your head everything you already knew about holidays, for example:

- Holidays often involve travel
- Holidays can be fun!
- Holidays can go wrong!

CAN YOU WRITE DOWN ANY MORE IDEAS THAT THE WORD 'HOLIDAYS' conjures up in your mind?

THE PRIOR KNOWLEDGE STRATEGY helps you to predict what might come up; it helps you to identify how the text you are listening to diverges from what you expected to come up.

The PRIOR KNOWLEDGE STRATEGY is one that EMI students can also use when listening to the teacher, to a video recording during the lesson, or to a podcast on the internet. HOWEVER BEWARE! Prior knowledge of a topic in an EMI lesson is very different to prior knowledge of a topic in an English language class. Can you think of some of the differences? Here is one to start you off:

Prior Knowledge in a General English Lesson	*Prior Knowledge in EMI Lesson*
The topic is usually familiar to the student, they will have at least some experience of it	The topic may be totally new to the student

MOREOVER, BE CAREFUL!!! There is a danger with the Prior Knowledge Strategy. You might *think* you are understanding something the teacher is saying by activating your Prior Knowledge of the topic. This may lead you to actually stop listening, or not listening attentively enough and then you may miss something important. So:

When listening to a topic, make sure you frequently ask yourself: *Does what the teacher is saying match my prior knowledge of the topic? Or is s/he saying something that maybe contradicts my prior knowledge of the topic?* After a while, this strategy should become automatic.

When listening to a lesson, try to activate the following strategies:

PREDICTING: as in the example of the holiday (above). But be careful about predicting what might come next when it is a new topic in your subject.

INFERENCING: You may be able to 'infer' the meaning of a new word or phrase that comes up in a lesson *from the context* in which it is uttered (spoken).

MONITORING: This will require high levels of concentration! Keep asking yourself: Am I understanding this? And if not, why not?

EVALUATING: This is where you 'stand back' from the listening process. So maybe you should do this during a break in the lesson or at the end. Ask yourself: should I be predicting more or less? Should I be trying to infer more? Or am I inferring too much? Am I taking notes in an efficient manner? (see Note-Taking pages in this book)

Prior Knowledge and the Different Subjects

Prior knowledge may even have a different role to play in different EMI subjects. Try to discuss this with fellow students (from your subject) together with students from other subjects. Here are some phrases to help you start off:

- New topics follow on from old topics
- New topics are completely new
- I know a bit about this topic anyway from my knowledge of the world
- I have already had personal experience of this topic
- We did this topic a bit in secondary school (High School)

Prior Knowledge, Listening Strategies and the Difficulty of the Task

Let's think about listening to the teacher as 'a task'. What do you bring to that task? Write down some thoughts here:

_____

Now look at the three figures with the title 'EMI Listening Tasks'

Figure 3.5.1 suggests that you bring, to the process of listening, your current knowledge of English, particularly your vocabulary and grammar. You also bring your knowledge of how lessons or lectures are normally conducted (this is sometimes called 'discourse knowledge'). You also bring what is called 'pragmatic knowledge' (how individuals put across a message in a particular way). You will also have some idea of the social and cultural behaviours of both teachers and students in that particular context. This may be especially important if you are an international student with perhaps a different social and cultural background. Available to you is also your 'strategic effort' – what you _will do_ with the linguistic knowledge that you have PLUS your prior knowledge of the topic.

Now, let's continue to think of listening to the teacher 'as a task'. Perhaps the task is relatively easy for you (Figure 3.5.2). For example, you have done this topic before; the teacher talks slowly and explains things clearly, gives examples, asks if you have understood, and you recognise most of the

EMI listening tasks

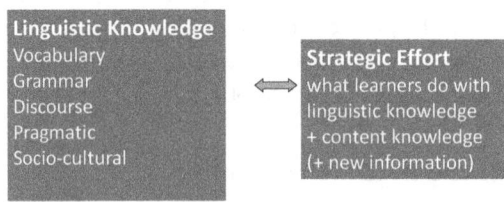

FIGURE 3.5.1 EMI Listening Task 1.

FIGURE 3.5.2 EMI Listening Task 2.

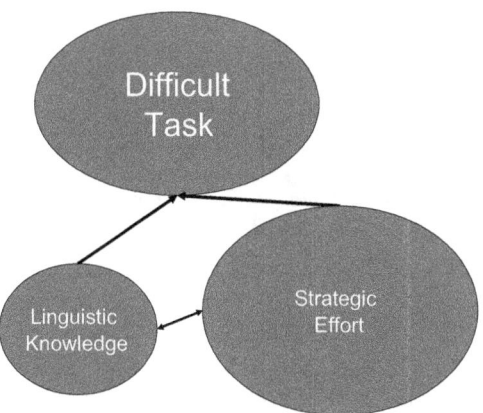

FIGURE 3.5.3 EMI Listening Tasks 3.

vocabulary that is being used. If the task is relatively easy, then your strategic effort will be quite low.

If, on the other hand, the task of listening is difficult (for example the teacher talks too fast; the topic is completely new; there are lots of new technical words with complex explanations, it's not clear how what s/he says matches what is on the slides), then you will have to increase your amount of strategic effort (Figure 3.5.3).

Having worked through this section on the strategy 'prior knowledge of the topic', will you change anything about the way you go about listening to the teacher? Write some thoughts here and also discuss them with a classmate.

___

3.6

THE IRF SEQUENCE

What It Is For; What It Does; How to Deal with It

> **GLOSSARY**
>
> *ubiquitous*   can be found everywhere, in many places or situations
> *impart*   to communicate

IRF stands for **INITIATION; RESPONSE; FEEDBACK**.
The IRF sequence is 'ubiquitous' in all aspects of education. Ubiquitous here means: *it can be found in all classrooms*, from primary school, through to EMI classrooms in universities. It is a tool that teachers use in order to impart knowledge, set up a kind of 'conversation' with the class, or check how much students know or have understood. Some people would say that it is also a tool for the teacher to 'keep control'!

Let's think about how the IRF sequence affects your learning in the EMI classroom.

Here are two <u>very simple</u> Initiation Response Feedback sequences in a Geography lesson:

(Sequence 1)

(I) Teacher: What is the capital of Nigeria?
(R) Student: Abuja
(F) Teacher: Yes, well done!

(Sequence 2)

(I) Teacher: What is the capital of Nigeria?
(R) Student: Lagos
(F) Teacher: No… well it used to be Lagos… but in the 1990s Abuja became the official capital of Nigeria.

QUESTION TO YOU: What is the teacher trying to do with these two IRFs here?

_____
_____

Here are two extracts from a Mathematics lecture:

Extract 1

Teacher: …divided by H you remember this, you remember this right? so er, what we have is that actually the same thing is happening just with with Y, frozen, ok?, that corresponds to what in this picture? <GRAPH ON SLIDE > it corresponds to, freezing, Y (with) Y zero ok?, and then looking how F increases or decreases along the direction of X ok? so this is the direction of X ok? <STILL INDICATING GRAPH> and so in this case we just spot what what would you expect that your partial derivative with respect to X is positive negative or you don't know, what do you expect?

Student: negative

Teacher: negative right? Because it goes down, ok?, there is a completely symmetrical definition for the derivative with respect to Y, which I show you next. there is this this here below <INDICATING SLIDE>.

Extract 2

Teacher: ….positive very well, so what i expect is this is, positive <WRITING ON IPAD>, ok?, ok, another question… estimate the value of F prime ok, at Q <READING EXERCISE ON SLIDE> ok? well we do you do the same thing for P well what happens…I don't write it but what happens for P? what i move erm to the right from P, I move to the right <INDICATING GRAPH ON SLIDE>. I move to the right, am I going towards increasing or decreasing levels of F?

Student:	increasing
Teacher:	increasing… so the partial derivative with respect to X is?
(same) Student:	positive
Teacher:	very well, and if I move towards the direction of Y? <INDICATING GRAPH ON SLIDE>, what we don't see any level curve right? There is nothing pictured.

Can you spot a difference in the use of the IRF in these two extracts? What is that difference?

___

Are these the kinds of sequences that you sometimes get in your subject classes? If your answer is 'yes', how do you feel about them? Are they useful? In what way?

___

Now let's look at a more 'extended IRF sequence' in a lesson about linguistics (the study of language). In what way do you think it is 'extended'?

Extract 3

Teacher:	So now we come on to the topic of the codification of language….What do we mean by the codification of language…anyone…anyone…yes?
Student:	speaking and writing properly?
Teacher:	Ok but what do you mean by speaking properly?
Student:	Using words like… in dictionary… or sentences in grammar books.
Teacher:	Ok but what is the process? How does a language become codified?
Student:	By people writing dictionaries and grammar books?
Teacher:	yes, that's the kind of thing…and so it becomes codified over…over a period….?
Student:	Over a period of time?
Teacher:	Yes exactly, over a period of time. So, let's now think…why might this be a problem….

How does the teacher extend the IRF sequence in Extract 3? What is the teacher trying to achieve by extending the IRF sequence? Could the teacher have made the sequence more like the IRF in Extracts 1 and 2? What would have been the effect on the student of making it shorter?

Finally let's look at Extract 4

Extract 4

Teacher:	I don't remember probably a mathematician called Hess invented it but I really... I should know but I don't erm, ok and it's what a matrix.... have you ever seen a matrix? in your life?
Students in chorus:	no
Teacher:	never?
Students in chorus:	no, no, never
Teacher:	you have a question?
Student:	erm from before... when I have y and x
Teacher:	when you have y and x, what?
Student:	er... the derivative of y xx
Teacher:	if you have... you mean this before <SHOWING PREVIOUS SLIDE) with respect to x and then with respect to y?
Student:	no afterwards
Teacher:	afterwards?
Student:	afterwards we have the xx
Teacher:	yeah yeah the this is the notation with this... yes you can you can...

Although Extract 4 above does not appear to have a typical IRF sequence, it does contain one of sorts...can you spot it? *Hint*: The student is asking for clarification and the teacher is......?

In your classes/lectures, how often does the IRF sequence (in all its different forms) appear? Put a circle around how often it appears:

1. very simple IRF (very often; often; rarely)
2. simple but slightly extended IRF (very often; often; rarely)
3. extended IRFIRF (very often; often; rarely)
4. Embedded/obscured IRF – Student Asking For Clarification, followed by IRF (very often; often; rarely)

Discuss with your classmates:

1) What are the advantages of more 'extended IRFs'? Are there disadvantages? If extended IRFs happen rarely in your classes, why do you think that is? _____
2) If your answers to some of the questions above were 'it depends', what does it depend on? For example, 'if it's revision of a topic then.....'
_____

3) In your class, are there some students who are asked questions more than others (we might call these 'go to students')? If so, why do you think that happens? If it happens, what are the advantages and disadvantages?
_____

WAIT TIME AND FEEDBACK. What is it for? What does it do? How are you going to deal with it?

Wait time is the length of silence following the *Initiation* by the teacher, or the length of silence following a student's *Response*.
 For example (Biology lesson):

Teacher: Yesterday I told you, a poison, do you remember? A poison for the mitotic fuse named? (*3 seconds wait time*), Clara, can you remember? (*2 seconds wait time*)
Clara: colchicina? (*1 second wait time*)
Teacher: colchicina, very good, very good, good student

For you to do: Ok so now let's think about <u>what happens during the wait time</u>. Write your thoughts here by finishing the sentences below:

- During the 3 seconds of wait time following the teacher's 'initiation', ...
- When the teacher nominates Clara there is a wait time of 2 seconds. During that time she ....
- After Clara's response, there is 1 second of wait time before the teacher confirms that the answer is correct. During that time Clara ....

What do you do when a teacher asks you a question?_____
 What does it depend on? Do you ever translate the question into your home language (L1)?
 Research suggests that (generally) teachers do not give more than 3 seconds wait time for students to provide an answer, after they have initiated a question. Why do you think this might be?

_____

FEEDBACK in class

What kind of feedback to an answer that you have given does your teacher provide? Any of the following? Check one or more of the boxes below. The teacher provides:

☐ A gloss (a short explanation) of the technical term *you* have used.
☐ A 're-voicing' of your answer (another way of saying it – perhaps using more technical language).
☐ A correction of what you have said in terms of the 'content' of your answer.
☐ A correction of what you have said in terms of the English that you have used (correcting your English).
☐ Other?

What do you do with the feedback you have received from the teacher during an oral exchange/sequence?

_____

If in class you make a note of the *feedback*, do you do so in English or in your home language? What would be the advantages of either?

The IRF Sequence/Teacher Questioning, and Pair/Group Work

How often in your classes does 'pair work' or 'group work' happen (for example the teacher asks the students to discuss a topic in pairs or in small groups before the teacher presents some related material).

In my class it happens:

☐ Often (for example, two or three times in every lesson)
☐ Occasionally (for example once in a lesson, usually at the beginning)
☐ Rarely
☐ Never
☐ We have special, separate 'group discussion' sessions, but in class we normally do not.

Write here what you think about pair/group work in class. For example, does it help you understand content?

_____

Now compare what you have written with one of your classmates. Do they have the same opinion?

_____

3.7

YOU AND YOUR HOME LANGUAGE

To Use or Not to Use, That Is the Question!

GLOSSARY

banned	not allowed
international student	a student from a different country who has come to study in the university
equivalents	the same, or as near as possible the same

Let's start off by reassuring you:

- There has been a lot of debate and research about this question!
- There is general agreement that the home language (L1) should not be banned from the EMI classroom.

BUT there is not a lot of agreement about:

- How much L1 should be used?
- For what purposes it should be used?
- Whether both teachers and students should use it
- What you should do when you have classmates who do not speak your home language well enough
- How much it helps or doesn't help students with their subject knowledge
- How much it stops students making progress with their English (Academic English in particular)

OH DEAR! That's the problem with research! Rarely a simple answer!

In an earlier section of this book, we raised the question of whether your EMI teachers use your home language. But of course that is not a very simple question to answer because:

1) You may be an international student who doesn't speak the majority language of the country you are studying in – at least not sufficiently well to study your subject in it
2) You may be a national of the country you are studying in but speak another of the languages of that country – *not the one the teacher speaks*
3) You may be either (1) or (2) but your teacher is not a native of your country and does not speak your home language sufficiently well to be able to code-switch to it.

Have we missed any other possibilities?_____

For you to do:
Over a week of classes/lectures make a rough list of:
How much, if any, home language is used by your EMI teacher(s)
What is it used for? For example:

- Home language (L1) equivalents for individual words (remember the 'Technical/academic/everyday language distinction);
- repetition of whole phrases/sentences (or longer) already spoken in English;
- translations into the home language of what is in English on the slides;
- repeating something in L1 when students signal they have not understood the English version.

What is your reaction to a teacher using your home language to teach aspects of your subject?

If they do use the home language, what 'do you do with it' – for example, make a written note; make a mental note.

Does your teacher ask you to do activities in student-groups? Are you expected to use only English? If so, why do you think that might be?

Now discuss what you have written with one or more of your classmates. Do you agree or disagree?

_____
_____

3.8

LANGUAGE DEMANDS OF NOTES

> **GLOSSARY**
>
> *crucial*   extremely important
> *chatty*   talkative, always chatting
> *abbreviations*   shortened forms of words, for example eng = engineering; bec=because
> *indented section*   part of a text that is moved in a little from the right side of the page
> *spatially*   in space/in two dimensions

You already have experience of making notes in your own language, but it is useful to think about note-taking in English and the challenges this may present.

Listening and In-Flight Note-Taking

It is very difficult to listen and write at the same time. It is natural that while you are listening carefully, you will not want to write, you will be concentrating on what is being said so will find note-taking a distraction. It is equally possible that while making notes you will miss some of what the lecturer says – you will be concentrating on writing so will not have the time to listen. Balancing listening time with note-taking time is crucial. It is also important to understand that even the best notes will be an incomplete record of a lecture.

Comprehension and In-Flight Note-Taking

It is probable that there will be times that you do not fully understand what is being said in a lecture. This is perfectly normal, so do not panic. Your notes are a preliminary step in the learning process and you can work on any gaps in understanding after the lecture. It is a good idea to mark your notes with a comment or symbol to indicate that you did not fully understand the content, so you can fix it later.

Make sure you sit in a good place to hear the lecturer clearly. Avoid sitting near chatty students or noisy air conditioning units!

Concentration and In-Flight Note-Taking

Making in-flight notes in an academic lecture is not easy! Most lectures last for approximately one hour and concentrating, in English, for all this time is tiring and probably unrealistic. So, understand that you may have moments when you miss what has been said and put this on your list of things to fix after the lecture.

Note-Taking and the Language You Use

Making notes requires attention and concentration. Writing in complete sentences is often very demanding so is best avoided. Instead, think about using key words, abbreviations or phrases and develop a repertoire of symbols for logical connections. Remember that notes are an aid to memory, not a transcript of the lecturer's words. The aim is to produce a document that can be improved and developed after the lecture. You do not have to get everything first time!

Note-Taking in Your First Language

It may be that, for convenience or speed, you occasionally wish to use your first language for note-taking. This is absolutely fine – but remember you will need to work out how to express these first language notes in English. It is important that you work out how often you use your first language and think about how it might benefit you and how it might give you problems.

Linear (or Outline) Notes: Language Demands and Advantages

This is the most common and perhaps most simple form of note-taking. Notes are organised chronologically with headings, numbers, letters and indented sections to structure the content. There are variations on this style, but essentially it is a chronological and organised record of the lecture content.

TITLE OF LECTURE

Date
1) Introduction
   a)
   b)
2) Section One
   a)
      i.
      ii.
3) Section Two

The Language Demands of Linear Notes

This style of note-taking often demands that you write in complete sentences or longer phrases. This language demand can slow you down and require a lot of thinking time. As a result, the danger is that you might miss some important content while focusing on your notes. It may be quicker and less demanding to use abbreviations, symbols and diagrams.

Advantages of Linear Notes

The advantage of this style is that it is probably very familiar to you. Linear notes are also more language-intensive, so will be a more useful language record of the lecture when you come to use them again.

Potentially Less Memorable

By representing the content of a lecture in written form, the content of the lecture is potentially less memorable than if diagrams or images are used. You may consider using different colours and fonts to help with this.

Spidergram (or Mind Map) Notes: Language Demands and Advantages

This is probably a familiar style of note-taking. Notes are organised by making connections between ideas, fact or concepts – rather than chronologically. Colours, arrows and symbols are common in this form of note-taking

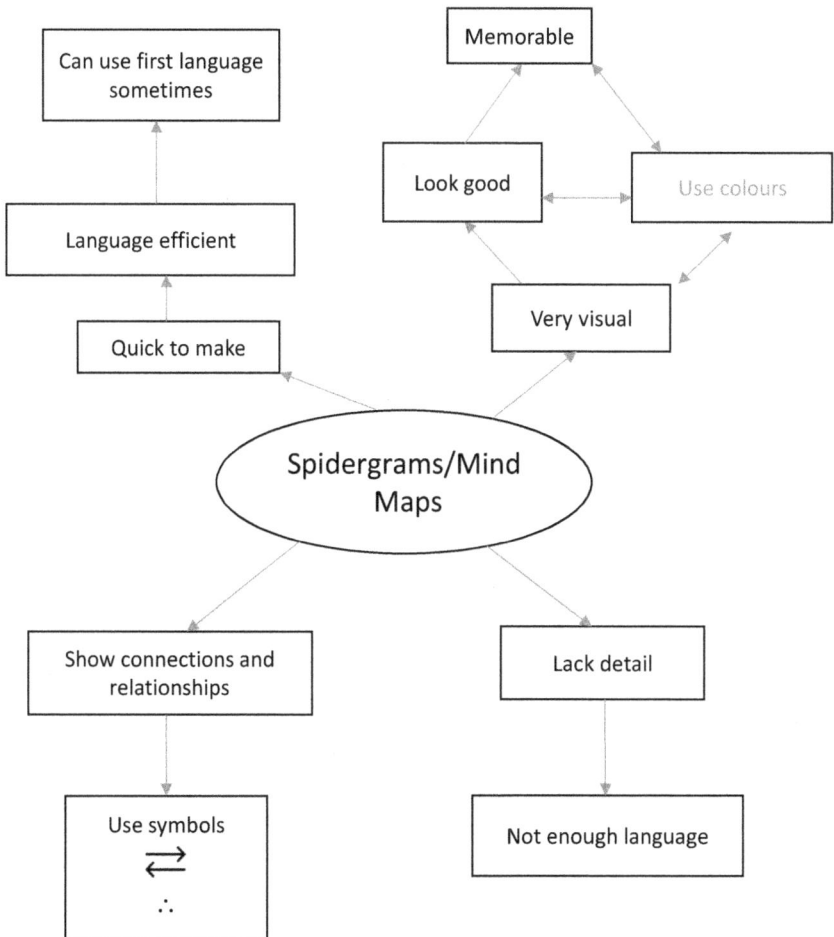

The Language Demands of Spidergram Notes

The disadvantage of these notes is connected to their advantages! The most appealing quality of these notes is that they are very quick to make as they have a relatively low language demand. They are also, visually, very accessible and quick to understand.

The disadvantage is that because of the relatively low language demand these notes may lack detail and so might give an incomplete record of the content. This will not be a problem while your memory of the lecture is fresh – but it may become problematic as your memory fades. Spidergrams or mind maps often work at the level of individual words or short phrases, and so do not involve longer, potentially useful strings of words. So, the language demand of these notes will come when you start to develop them and transform them into assessed work.

Advantages of Spidergrams

Spidergrams are quick to make, visually appealing and familiar. They are often pleasing to make and because they work spatially, allow you to work out relationships between ideas or concepts. They are also easier to compare with classmates as they are relatively quick to digest and understand. Because of their format, you should be able to add to them and adapt them for a second, more complete draft.

CHAPTER 4
AROUND YOUR CLASSES
REFLECTING AFTER LANDING

4.1
IMPROVING YOUR NOTE-TAKING TOGETHER

> **GLOSSARY**
>
> *flip chart paper*   very large sheets of paper used during presentations
> *marker pen*   a thick pen used to write on a flip chart
> *collaborative*   working together

It is important to think of your in-flight notes as the first draft or first attempt, which can be improved. You may have missed some of the content of the lecture or may have only partly understood some of the lecturer's words. Here are some ideas to help you:

Work Together to Improve then Develop Your Notes

'Flip' Your Notes Together – first steps in collective sense making

For this exercise you will need some flip chart paper (or the equivalent) some coloured marker pens and two or three classmates. Each of you will have a different coloured pen. The idea is that working together you create a really good version of notes for the lecture you have just attended on the flip paper. Use any style you wish – but mind-maps/spider-grams work really well.

DOI: 10.4324/9781003544241-30

One Note – sense making in digital space

It is not always possible to be in the same room together so it is helpful to explore digital options for collective note-making. Use an application such as Microsoft OneNote to create collective notes. You can also use free to use online applications such as Padlet (2024) to create interesting and memorable collective notes.

Google Docs – another digital space option

This is another easily accessible collaborative document application. It is very popular as it is very intuitive and integrates well into your current digital space.

When you have finished, take a photograph (or screenshot) or save the collaborative document. If you have made a mind map – it is important that you continue to work on the language needed to explain or articulate the content as clearly as you can. You need to transform the notes into connected speech. Consider Cornell notes as a good transition instrument – the need for summary writing is especially useful.

References

Padlet (2024) Available at: padlet.com (Accessed 15 July 2024).

4.2
THE POWER OF TALKING

> **GLOSSARY**
>
> | | |
> |---|---|
> | *to overestimate* | to regard as more important than it really is |
> | *linear* | formed one after the other in a line |
> | *sequential* | ordered in a logical sequence |
> | *sense making* | the process of finding meaning or understanding something |
> | *to articulate* | to express clearly in words |

It is almost impossible to overestimate the importance of talking in your learning process. 'Putting things into words' is not only how you express your understanding of the world, it is also your most important tool for trying to make sense of the world.

If you think about it, language is by its very nature linear and sequential; it is ordered and organised. Your thoughts or the difficult things you have recently learnt are often not ordered and organised in your head – so expressing them in language is a way of finding an order and organisation for your thoughts.

This is not easy, and you may need to work with others to achieve the clarity you are seeking. By talking about your course content, you will quickly find out what you can and cannot express clearly. If you cannot put something into words, it is probable that either you do not have the content clear in your mind or that you do not yet have the language needed to articulate the content. This is a clear sign that you need to do something about it!

Working and talking together is a means of sense making; it is a process of using language to better understand and express the content of your course. It is a way of working together to 'fill in the gaps', of finding ways to express ideas and thoughts in language appropriate to your academic subject.

Talking and 'putting into words' is a key tool for developing your understanding and for practising the language you need for your course. It is absolutely crucial!

If you think about this carefully, you will know that at university you are not tested on what you know – but on what you can express in language, what you can articulate in English. It is, therefore, very important that you practise putting your understanding into English.

Fortunately, there are many ways you can do this! We will explore some of them in sections below.

4.3

WORK WITH COURSEMATES

From Notes to Connected Speech

> **GLOSSARY**
>
> *solitary*　　　alone
> *unstructured*　with no organisation

Sense making by talking is not necessarily a solitary process. You can do a lot of really important work with your classmates after the lecture. Naturally, some of this may be informal and relatively unstructured, and it might even be fun!

Informal Sense Making

You may, for example, go for a coffee together and chat about the lecture. You might ask each other for your understanding of any difficult points or for anything that was not clear to you. This is all good! With limited access to your teachers, it is very important that you help each other even if it is very informal.

We Don't Just Remember Things – We Remember How and Where We Learn Them

We are not just information processors – we are human beings. Our memory captures a huge amount of data including emotions, sights, sounds and circumstances. Sense making with friends can really help you to understand and remember course content, as we will remember how we learnt it. We will remember the laughter and the frustrations; we will remember the place where we sat and talked – all of these things will make the course content more memorable!

If You Want to be a Little More Formal

You may, however, wish to develop this peer-to-peer sense making into something a little more formal or structured. Here are some ideas you might wish to try. The following sections offer you some ideas to improve your sense making with classmates.

4.4

ACCOUNTABLE TALK

Making It All a Little More Formal

> **GLOSSARY**
>
> *accountable*   responsible, having to explain and give reasons
> *formalising*   making more formal, more academic
> *essentially*   fundamentally
> *progression*   a natural continuation

Logical Connections

Accountable talk, Wolf, Crossen and Resnick (2006), is a way of formalising your learner talk by focussing on logical connections between ideas, facts or opinions. Essentially, it is a formal summary technique in which you focus on key connecting words such as:

Because
Consequently
Therefore
So
But
However

> **Task**: Make a short list of other connecting words or phrases in English.

Your challenge is to make a spoken summary of your notes, concentrating on the logical connections between statements, ideas or concepts. Your classmates listen carefully and then produce their own spoken summaries one at a time – they work from their own notes but can use anything from any previous summary to help them. The idea is that the summaries gradually improve! Listen and learn!

This technique focusses on the power of language to organise thinking and to establish logical connections between ideas. It uses logical connecting words to highlight this effort.

Other People's Thoughts and Ideas

This is a progression from the previous exercise! You must continue to make logical connections, but this time you need to make a special effort to refer to the opinions and thoughts of others. This could be the contributions of your coursemates or, more formally, ideas or thoughts from your reading or lectures.

Try using phrases such as:

> X suggested that …
> X argues that …
> According to X, …
> X's ideas are very useful here because …

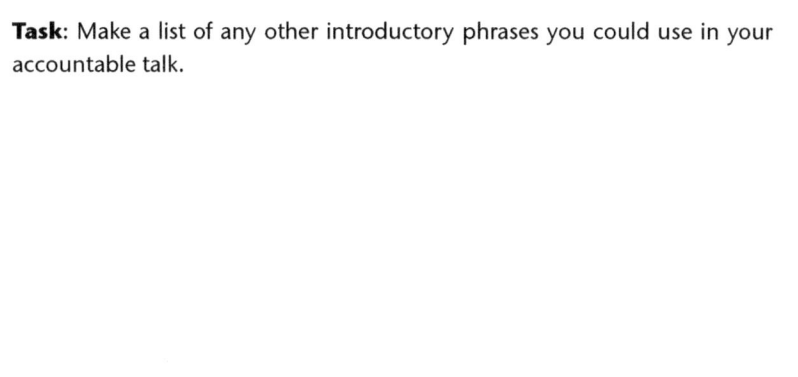

References

Wolf, M.K., Crossen, A. C. and Resnick, L.B. (2006) *Accountable talk in reading comprehension discussion.* CSE Technical Report, 670. Los Angeles. Learning and Research Development Centre, University of Pittsburgh.

4.5
MULTIWORD UNITS

These are also known as: 'FORMULAS' or 'LEXICAL BUNDLES' or 'FORMULAIC PHRASES' or 'COLLOCATIONS'. Yes, we know, linguists sometimes just can't make decisions!

Multiword units are used a lot in human speech and writing. Some of them just make communication faster and easier. For others, it's difficult to say why these 'combinations of words' are used because very often there is a perfectly good word that does the job equally well. For example, the phrase '*I'm over the moon*' means:

I'm very happy,
I'm delighted,
I'm ecstatic (about this).

But we seem to often prefer something a bit more unusual, something a bit more 'metaphoric'. In fact, it's not always easy to distinguish multiword units from metaphors.

By the way, we hope you're *over the moon* about this book!

- Here is an extract from an English newspaper (The Guardian online, 13 June 2024) which, as a student, you might find interesting to read anyway. Try to identify any multiword units in it. Are you sure you know what they all mean?

    Due to the cost of living crisis, more than half of full-time students are working long hours in jobs to support themselves at university, spending nearly two days a week in paid employment during term time. A survey of 10,000 full-time UK undergraduates by the Higher Education Policy Institute (HEPI) found a record 56% had paid employment while they were studying, working an average of 14.5 hours each week.

Experts said that the lack of maintenance support was creating a two-tier higher education system, with a widening divide between students who need to work long hours to survive while their better-off peers are free to concentrate on their studies and improve their grades.

When combined with time spent attending lectures, classes and other study, students with part-time jobs are averaging 48-hour working weeks during term time, while some have 56-hour weeks – far above the average 36.6 hours by adults in full-time jobs, according to the Office for National Statistics.

Rose Stephenson, Hepi's director of policy, said the traditional model of higher education, with undergraduates studying full-time away from home, was becoming unattainable unless student maintenance support was improved.

Stephenson said: 'As students battle the cost of living, the trend around part-time work becomes more concerning. Most students work and the number of hours they work is increasing, and if this trend continues full-time study may become unfeasible for many Adams (2024).

"The UK prides itself on its traditional, full-time residential study model for many students, with high completion rates. There's a chance that without intervention, the higher education model may accidentally evolve ... into a two-tier system based on who can afford to attend university."

The cost of living crisis abruptly flipped the proportion of students mixing paid employment and full-time study. Before 2021, roughly two-thirds of students had no paid employment in term time. But this year, 56% of students said they had paid employment and were working longer hours than students in previous years.

Three-quarters of those in work said they did so to meet their living costs, while 23% also said they worked to give financial support for friends or family.

"For a lot of students, paid employment isn't a choice, it's something they have to do," Stephenson said.

- Here is a transcription from the beginning section of a lecture on English Medium Instruction. Try to identify any multi-word units used by the lecturer.

In this introductory presentation, I am going to attempt to establish where, up to the present day, the research on English Medium Instruction (EMI) has been carried out – in other words, in which countries. I'm going to make a stab at doing this in relation to the broader fields of Applied Linguistics and Education. I am going to focus down on three aspects of this 'situating of EMI': Who and where are the participants; in what ways, if any, does EMI overlap with English for Academic Purposes (EAP) and English for Specific Purposes)? and who is carrying out the research in EMI?

Some authors who have used the term EMI have argued that it should be expanded to include Anglophone countries. This has been countered by Rose et al (2021), among others, because of its lack of equivalence historically, lack of equivalence in English language admission requirements, and lack of equivalence in policy making. My own position is that EMI should not include Anglophone countries.

EAP/ESP research has predominantly been located in Anglophone countries (particularly USA, UK, Australia, Canada). Moreover, and importantly, the largest number of studies that we looked at were 'corpus-based' or 'desk-based' research studies – in other words not located in any particular country. By contrast, the vast majority of EMI studies were indeed located in non-Anglophone countries (Spain, China, Hong Kong, Turkey etc). In fact, we only located two studies, that described themselves as EMI, in the USA and Canada.

- In this book, we have asked you to record a portion of a lesson taught by one of your teachers. Identify some of the multiword phrases used by your teacher in that lesson. Are they obvious (easy to understand)? Or are they obscure (difficult to understand)? Were they more frequent or less frequent than in the transcriptions we gave you (above)?

_____
_____
_____
_____

References

Richard Adams. "More than half of UK students working long hours in paid jobs" The Guardian, 13 June 2024, https://www.theguardian.com/education/article/2024/jun/13/more-than-half-of-uk-students-working-long-hours-in-paid-jobs#:~:text=The%20cost%20of%20living%20crisis%20abruptly%20flipped%20the%20proportion%20of,than%20students%20in%20previous%20years

4.6
WORD FAMILIES

Here is a word that is often used in academic disciplines:

FREQUENT

Here are words that are associated with the word 'frequent':

Infrequent	Infrequently	Frequency
Frequently	Frequencies	Frequentative
	Frequentness	Frequented

All these words make up a 'word family'.

Think of a 'technical word' in your own subject *in a recent lesson* that is a member of a word family.

Try to find out <u>how many</u> members of that word family there are. You can use the internet to help you: simply try typing different versions of that word.

DOI: 10.4324/9781003544241-35

How does the meaning of the original word change according to each of the members of the family?
_____
_____
_____

In other parts of this book, we have talked about the 'strategies' that you as an EMI student can use. 'Playing around' with word families is a strategy that might be useful to you. Do you do this already? Write down how and when you use this strategy, then share it with a classmate:
_____
_____
_____
_____

4.7
GENTLY PERSUADING YOUR TEACHERS

Get together with some of your fellow students – the ones who have *attended at least some* of the same lessons as you.

For some of the items below, you may need to refer to other sections in this book where you will have been given an explanation of the terms being used.

Discuss how you could go about <u>gently and politely</u> encouraging your teacher(s) to:

1. Check students' understanding more often.
2. Ask students more often if they want something repeated or repeated using different words.
3. Identify clearly for students which words are *technical words* - those that are *a label* for a concept, idea, or perspective in an academic subject.
4. Use more and clearer *discourse markers* so that students better follow the narrative of the lesson.
5. (and connected to 4) encourage the teacher to provide some material in advance of the lesson with opportunities for students to ask questions about the material at the start of the lesson.
6. Explain the relationship between what they are saying and what they have written on slides or notes/handouts.
7. Suggest to students how they might use more learning strategies or use the current ones better.
8. Be aware that there are many 'different types' of students in the class. This could be cultural/national differences, language proficiency differences or 'different transition patterns' from secondary (high school) education to university.

DOI: 10.4324/9781003544241-36

4.8

ELABORATE INTERROGATION

How/Why?

> **GLOSSARY**
>
> *moreover* in addition
> *restrict* limit, prevent from doing more

Making questions about a lecture you have just attended can be a very helpful way of clarifying your thinking. Moreover, listening to classmates answer your questions can really help with your sense making.

In this exercise, based on Elaborate Interrogation, Dunlowsky et al. (2013), you only use *how* and *why* questions to focus and restrict your thinking. Try it – it's not easy, but it is very useful!

How
Why

This is a two-part exercise. Formulating How and Why questions makes you think hard about the content, while answering them puts the focus on the language you need.

- *How* questions focus on processes and sequences and may require detailed descriptive answers.
- *Why* questions may focus on causes or reasons and so require detailed explanation.

To give an increased challenge, you could use the discipline of *accountable talk* described in Section 4 above.

Task: Think of a recent lecture and write three questions beginning How and three questions beginning Why.

Additional Task: Whether working alone or with classmates, make notes on how you would answer the questions. Think carefully about the language you need to express yourself clearly. You may wish to refer to the sections that follow.

References

Dunlosky, J., Rawson, K.A. and Marsh, E.J. (2013) Improving students' learning with effective learning techniques, *Psychological Science in the Public Interest* 14.1. Available at: https://bit.ly/3jsll7w (Accessed: 15 July 2024).

4.9
GUIDED RECIPROCAL PEER QUESTIONING

The Power of Questions and Answers!

GLOSSARY

reciprocal   involving both parties equally
peer   people of the same level or status, here – classmates

It is generally agreed that EMI learners should be challenged by doing difficult tasks. It is also agreed that questioning and answering have a key role in the sense making process. This exercise develops the Q&A techniques of the previous exercise adapted from King (1990). It is a small group exercise that is both quite difficult but could be highly rewarding.

Task: After a lecture get together and, working alone for a few minutes, try to complete at least four of the question cues below with questions about the lecture you have just attended.

Explain why _____.
Explain how _____.
What is the meaning of _____?
Why does _____ happen?
What is the main idea of _____?

What is the solution to the problem of _____?
What if _____?
What conclusions can I make about _____?
What is the best _____ and why?
What do you think causes _____? Why?
How does _____ affect _____?
How does _____ relate to what I've learnt before?
What is the difference between _____ and _____?
How are _____ and _____ similar?
How would I use _____ to _____?
What are the strengths and weaknesses of _____?
What is another way to look at _____?
What is a new example of _____?
Why is _____ important?
How does _____ apply to everyday life?

Task: When you are ready, take it in turns to ask your questions – ask classmates (who may try to answer using the accountable talk techniques!). Help each other to improve the content and language of your answers.

References

King, A. (1990) Reciprocal peer-questioning: A strategy for teaching students how to learn from lectures, *The Clearing House*, 64(2) 131–135. http://www.jstor.org/stable/30188588 (Accessed: 15 July 2024).

4.10

REFLECTING ON QUESTIONS POST-LESSON

GLOSSARY

perception   the ability to see/hear/become aware, of something.
intelligibility   how possible it is to 'make out' a bit of speech.

---

1) WRITE DOWN ANY THREE QUESTIONS THAT *OTHER* STUDENTS HAVE ASKED IN A LESSON:

   1. _____
   2. _____
   3. _____

Why do you think they asked those questions? (Please don't write 'because they didn't understand what the teacher was saying' – that's too obvious! Try to go a bit deeper!)

What exactly do you think they did not understand?

2) If <u>you</u> asked a question in a lesson, write it here: _____
_____

Now try to think back why <u>you</u> asked that question.

   1. Was it a *language* problem? What kind?
   2. Was it a *perception* problem (you couldn't make out what the teacher was saying)?

3. Was it an *intelligibility* problem (perhaps the way that the teacher was pronouncing the word(s) was not familiar to you)?
4. Was it difficult to *follow an explanation*? (too complex; too many words; too fast)?

Now try to think about the differences between the difficulties in (1), (2), (3) and (4). Which problem comes up most often for you? Why do you think that is?

_____
_____
_____

3) Now write down any questions that you wish <u>you had</u> asked in that lesson (or any other lesson) but didn't. _____
_____
_____

Think back: Why did you not ask that question? What was the reason that you might have wanted to ask that question?

Now go back to one or two of the questions that your classmates asked that you wrote down above? Why do you think they asked those questions?

As usual, try to discuss this issue with one or more of your classmates.

4.11

EXAMPLES OF SOCRATIC QUESTIONS

Invitations to Better Thinking

> **GLOSSARY**
>
> | | |
> |---|---|
> | *taxonomy* | a list organised into categories or types |
> | *stimulating* | interesting, making you think |
> | *thought-provoking* | making you think because interesting or new |
> | *probe* | question deeply |
> | *assumptions* | things that are believed to be true without supporting evidence |
> | *distinctions* | differences between things or ideas/concepts |
> | *implications* | outcomes or possible results/conclusions |
> | consistency | regularity, with no contradictions |

Fisher (2003) developed the following taxonomy of question types and examples based on the inquiry models of Socrates. You may find the taxonomy and examples stimulating and thought-provoking. Indeed, Fisher's categories may well help you further develop yours! Fisher's fundamental idea is that questions are invitations to better thinking! Use the table below to develop your repertoire of questions and perhaps to improve your thinking! You could use this to further develop previous techniques based on questions and answers.

Questions that seek clarification	Purpose
Can you explain that? What do you mean by …? Can you give me an example of …? How does that help …? Does anyone have a question to ask about …?	Explaining, Defining Giving examples, Supporting, Enquiring
Questions that probe reasons and evidence	*Purpose*
Why do you think that …? How do we know that …? What are your reasons for …? Do you have any evidence of..? Can you give me an example of/a counter- example of …?	Forming an argument, Assumptions, Reasons, Evidence Examples/Counter-examples
Questions that explore alternative views	*Purpose*
Can you put it another way? Is there another point of view? What if someone were to suggest that …? What would someone who disagreed with you say? What's the difference between those views/ideas	Re-stating a view, Speculation, Alternative views, Counter-argument, Distinctions
Questions that test implications and consequences	*Purpose*
What follows from what you say? Does it agree with what was said earlier? What would be the consequences of …? Is there a general rule for that? How could you test to see if that were true?	Implications, Consistency, Consequences, Generalising rules, Testing for truth
Questions about the question/discussion	*Purpose*
Do you have a question about that? What kind of question is that? How does what you said or the question help us? What have we got so far/can we summarise? Are we any closer to answering the question?	Questioning, Analysing, Connecting, Summarising, Concluding

Fisher (2003: 154–5)

- Task: Use the table above to develop two more questions from each category. The questions could be about a recent lecture or reading text. Write your questions below.

_____
_____
_____
_____
_____
_____

- Task: Choose two or three of your questions from the previous exercise and think about how you might answer them. Write a short transcript of your answers below:

_____
_____
_____
_____
_____
_____

References

Fisher, R. (2003) *Teaching Thinking*. London: Continuum.

4.12

IDEAS FOR BETTER ANSWERS

> **GLOSSARY**
>
> *tips*   useful ideas or suggestions

It is helpful to think of your spoken answers as both content and language events. As such, every opportunity to answer a question is an opportunity to work on your content knowledge and an opportunity to practise your subject language.

Here are some tips for better answers:

o Listen to the question very carefully.
o Work out exactly what the lecturer is asking.
o Don't be afraid to ask the lecturer to repeat or rephrase the question if you need clarification or a little more time to think.
o Avoid one-word or short-phrase responses.
o Try to answer as fully as possible.
o Try to use relevant technical and academic vocabulary in your answers.
o Refer to your written notes when answering the question.
o Refer to your written notes when answering the question.
o Refer to previous lectures/classes if appropriate.
o Use the discipline of *accountable talk* to refer to the ideas of others and to refer to your reading.
o If appropriate, use your response to practise your *critical thinking*.

DOI: 10.4324/9781003544241-41

- o Don't be afraid to use your answer to explore other possible answers.
- o After the lecture, work on how you might improve your answers to any questions.
- o When others are answering questions imagine how you would answer the question yourself.
- o If a classmate gives a good answer, make a quick note of it – notice any technical or academic language.
- o After the lecture chat with any classmates who gave particularly good answers, find out more about their understanding of the question.

- **Task**: Choose six of the above tips and try to use them to improve your answers over the next semester. Notice how fantastic your answers become!

4.13

DEVELOPING YOUR RANGE OF RHETORICAL FUNCTIONS

> **GLOSSARY**
>
> *rhetorical*   referring to formal speaking
> *inventory*   a complete list of contents

Teachers sometimes refer to the language students use as *learner talk*. It is important to know this because there have been many efforts to describe exactly what learner talk is. Knowing what learner talk consists of can give you a structure for developing your own English learner talk – which will allow you to better use English in all the formal and informal settings where talking is required.

It is better not to describe the language you need at university as an inventory of grammar items, as the list would very quickly become very long and very confusing. A much better approach is to think about the communication jobs you will need to perform. This is similar to the phrase book approach. When on holiday in a country with an unfamiliar language you may well have used a phrase book to help you with some basic communication tasks. You might, for example, have used the phrase book to ask where the nearest bank is or to ask a waiter if there is a free table for two people. These communication tasks are often called rhetorical functions.

Learner talk consists of a wide range of rhetorical functions.

It is impossible to make a list of everything you could say in English, but we can list some of the most important things you need to do in English. Here is a preliminary list of high-frequency rhetorical functions:

o narrate events
o explain
o instruct
o ask different kinds of questions
o receive, act and build upon answers
o analyse and solve problems
o speculate and imagine
o explore and evaluate ideas
o discuss
o argue, reason and justify
o negotiate

Task: Reflect on your own English. Can you do the above things confidently and fluently? Do you need to further develop your language skills in these areas?

Developing Your Range of Rhetorical Functions (1)

- **Task**: Look at this link: http://www.uefap.com/speaking/spkfram.htm You will find another list of rhetorical functions with examples and language notes Gillet (2024).

o Combine the list above with this list.
o Look at the examples and the language used for each of the functions in the list from the link. Notice and make notes of any language that is new for you.
o Be prepared to use the new language in your own English language learner talk.

Developing Your Range of Rhetorical Functions (2)

- **Task**: Look at this link: https://www.eapfoundation.com/speaking/presentations/language/. Here you will find some rhetorical functions specific to giving academic presentations Smith (2020).

o Look at this webpage carefully.
o Check you can perform all the functions confidently and fluently!

Developing Your Range of Rhetorical Functions (3)

- **Task**: Look at this link https://www.phrasebank.manchester.ac.uk. Here you will find a resource primarily for academic writing – but its taxonomy of rhetorical functions is incredibly useful and much more specific University of Manchester (2023).

o Look at this website carefully. Do not try to learn everything!
o Use the website as a resource to help you think about a greater range of rhetorical functions. Remember that this resource is primarily for writing and that realising the functions in spoken language may require some changes. It is also worth remembering that different academic disciplines may have different language conventions for the functions.
o As your course progresses, notice how your lecturers realise the different functions.

References

Gillet, A. (2024) *UEFAP.com*. Available at: https://www.uefap.org (Accessed 15 July 2024).

Smith, S. (2020) eapfoundation.com. Available at: https://www.eapfoundation.com (Accessed 15 July 2024).

University of Manchester (2023) *Academic Phrasebank*. Available at: https://www.phrasebank.manchester.ac.uk (Accessed 15 July 2024).

4.14

WORKING ON YOUR OWN WITH YOUR SMARTPHONE

Smartphones give you the ability to record your voice using a voice recording app. This provides a wonderful opportunity for you to practise talking about your subject. Try this very useful and challenging exercise in transforming your notes into connected speech.

You could try this exercise alone after a lecture to practise summary techniques or with your classmates after working on *accountable talk* or *reciprocal peer questioning*. You may also find it a useful way of confirming how to express certain ideas, concepts or relationships before moving into tasks requiring writing.

A Basic Post-Lecture Smartphone Routine:

- Read through your notes a few times, concentrating on how you would summarise them in spoken form.
- Record a spoken summary of your notes, concentrating on clarity and accurate vocabulary.
- Listen to your spoken recording critically. What do you need to do to improve the recording? Could you be more fluent? If so, how could you achieve this?
- Delete
- Re-record your spoken version, concentrating on using good connecting language.
- Listen again.
- Review again, focussing on rhetorical functions.

- Delete
- Re-record.
- Reflect on any gaps in your language or subject knowledge. Make a note of these gaps and use them to help you focus on areas for development.

Using Your Smartphone to Develop Spoken Fluency (More Difficult!)

- Record a three-minute summary of your most recent lecture. (Use notes if you wish)
- Listen critically to your recording, thinking of how you would improve it.
- Delete your first recording.
- Make a second recording of only two minutes trying to cover the same content.
- Listen critically to your second recording, thinking of how you would improve it.
- Delete your second recording.
- Make a third recording of only one minute!
- Listen critically to your third recording, thinking of how you would improve it!

Note: This example uses 3 minutes; two minutes and one minute for the different iterations. You can use different timings – for example – one minute, 45 seconds and 30 seconds.

Record and Listen to Difficult Texts

- If you are having difficulty with part of a written text, record it on your smartphone.
- Go for a walk and listen to the recording a number of times.
- When you are ready, try to make your own spoken version of the difficult text.
- Use some of the techniques above to really practise hard!

4.15

MODIFIED CORNELL NOTES

From In-Flight Note-Taking to Post-Flight Note-Making

> **GLOSSARY**
>
> *Cornell* a university in America where this form of note-taking was first developed

When making in-flight notes, you need to be quick! Your notes are made in real time and the pressure is on. Because of this, linear notes and spidergrams are efficient and reliable ways of recording lecture content. However, after the lecture, we have the opportunity to improve these notes and make them work really well for us Cornell University (2024). In other words, note-taking can now become note-making.

Look at this template:

Headings	*Improved Notes*

Summary so far

This form of note-making is known as Cornell Notes. Use the headings column to better organise your notes into logical sections or paragraphs. Your in-flight notes may be a little messy, so this is the chance to tidy them up. You can now think carefully about your note-making, as you may well have worked with classmates to make sense of the content of the lecture.

When writing the summary, try to use the technical vocabulary of your discipline. Also, take care to express the ideas clearly in your own words. This is challenging but very important. You may wish to use the smartphone exercises to help you with this. Do not worry about perfection at this stage! The important thing is to get a basic version of your summary done and ready for improvement at a later stage.

References

Cornell University (2024) *The Cornell Note Taking System*. Available at: https://lsc.cornell.edu/how-to-study/taking-notes/cornell-note-taking-system/ (Accessed: 15 July 2024).

4.16

POST-CLASS READING FOR WRITING

Having completed your pre-reading and attended your class, reading now moves into a new stage: post-class reading for writing.

Here, writing may be an assignment or paper with a deadline in the current semester, or it may be writing required for examinations at the end of the semester or even at the end of the course. In any case, the end point of your reading activities will usually be written work of some form.

Reverse-Engineer Your Reading Work: Read with the End in Mind

> **Task:** Think about the written assignment you are reading for and consider these ten points:
>
> 1. When is the deadline for the assignment?
> 2. How much time have I got?
> 3. What is the title of the written assignment?
> 4. What key points/content are required of the title?
> 5. What do I already know?
> 6. What do I need to know?
> 7. Where can I find the new information that I need?
> 8. How much of the required reading is available online?
> 9. How much of the required reading requires visits to the library?
> 10. What level of detail do I need? General points or detailed argument?
> 11. What form of note-taking would work best for this assignment?

DOI: 10.4324/9781003544241-45

Keep your Assignment in Mind

From now on, you must be very focused on your reasons for reading. You are reading to answer a question – so you need to start collecting more information and content to answer the question as well as you can.

Break the Big Question into Smaller Questions

As in Section 4.11 above, you can break the big assignment question into smaller, more manageable questions. Spend some time developing a spider-gram of sub-questions. This can really help you to work out exactly what is required to answer the question well.

What Does Good Look Like?

Ask yourself what a good example of this assignment looks like. Think about:

- The macro-organisation of the assignment
- The language required
- The level of supporting detail
- The key sources/evidence or thinkers you need to refer to

Make a Preliminary Assignment Plan – Fill in the Gaps!

The more detailed your plan, the better your final written version will be. So, start now. Making a detailed plan will reveal the gaps in your knowledge and help you to make a really good structure for your answer. It will also tell you what you need to read! Regard your plan as a developing guide for your post-class reading. Don't be afraid to change or reorganise it in the light of new knowledge.

Make a note of the texts you need to read and where to find them. Compare with classmates and get busy!

4.17
WRITING

Summary Writing as a Transition to Writing

1. **A note about writing in English!**
   It is agreed that writing is an *iterative* process – that is, a process requiring multiple, improving drafts or versions until the finished draft is achieved. In-flight notes are the first step in this process; improved/enhanced notes are an important second step, while draft summary writing is the next stage in transforming notes into more formal academic writing.
2. **A note about writing in discipline!**
   Writing an academic paper/essay in your academic discipline means understanding how this is usually done. Of course, it will require a good use of technical vocabulary – but it is much more than this. There are conventions applied to the structure and organisation of written papers as well as to the language that is used. As far as possible, you need to immerse yourself in these conventions so you better understand what is required.

Summary Writing – A Fundamental Academic Comprehension and Output Skill

The ability to produce good summaries of academic content is a key skill and is fundamental to so many assessed tasks. Both formal written papers and spoken presentations will require you to produce summaries of ideas, theories, approaches and complex information – so it is worth practising!

It is also very important to recognise that producing a summary is a vital comprehension strategy when listening or reading. In-flight, 'up-to-now' mental summaries are vital in the comprehension process as they allow us to understand what we have listened to so far and, therefore, help us to anticipate and better comprehend what comes next.

As such, summarising is both a comprehension or processing technique and a formal written/spoken discipline. We have looked at some in-flight summarising techniques above – so let's now consider some techniques to help you develop this key skill in transforming notes into formal academic writing and speaking.

Summary Writing – More Ideas and Techniques

1. Three-word summaries: Think of three key words that recall the content of a recent lecture. (You could also use simple expressions). It is really helpful to compare with a classmate and to explain or justify why you chose your words or phrases. This is a pre-writing approach designed to help clarify your thinking!
2. One-sentence summaries: Try to summarise a section of the lecture in one simple sentence! Try to use your own words! This is more difficult than you might think! If it helps, try doing this exercise in your first language and then translating into English.
3. 10-second spoken summary: The same as above, but you record your voice! (As in the smartphone exercises, you could delete and repeat as necessary!)
4. Use the lecture title in a mind map summary: When the lecture has finished use the lecture title as the starting point for a mind map summary in note form.
5. Tweet summaries: Use Twitter (X) to tweet summaries to each other!
6. Lecture Outline: After the lecture, prepare a plan of the lecture outlining the key sections and important content. Getting the macro structure can really help when it comes to filling in the details!
7. Two-minute Co-construction: After the lecture has finished get together with a coursemate and together try to remember everything in chronological order. Make quick notes if you wish.
8. Five key technical words: Select five key technical words from the lecture and use them to organise your recollection of the lecture content.

Successful EMI academic writers spend more time planning than unsuccessful EMI academic writers. This indicates that the prewriting stages are especially important for you.

Writing Frames

Using a writing frame or skeleton is a very useful technique, as it can be designed with varying degrees of detail and complexity.

Look at this generic example:

ARGUMENT ESSAY – FRAME

Introduction

In this part of the essay, I need to demonstrate my approach to the subject and indicate my main argument or thesis statement.

Body

In this part of the essay, which may cover several paragraphs, I need to develop my argument by proposing supporting arguments – which must link to my main position.

I need to provide evidence and examples to support what I write – don't forget to think critically and evaluate the evidence.

I may also wish to present opposing views/evidence which I should also evaluate – perhaps negatively.

Continue this process until I am satisfied that I have made a strong case.

Conclusion

Briefly summarise my arguments and evidence with a final evaluation – this should be done to reinforce the position you took in your introduction. I may also wish to use a final *killer* argument/piece of evidence.

List of References

List only the sources I have referred to in my assignment.

Notes: In this essay, avoid using first-person pronouns such as I, me, my etc. Try to use hedging devices such as modal verbs to express degrees of commitment to the propositional content in your essay. Pay attention to the organisation and content of your paragraphs. (You may wish to refer to UEFAP.com or Academic Phrasebank).

Writing **121**

> **Task: Design a Writing Frame**
>
> Choose a recent or current writing assignment. Design a writing frame including details specific to the assignment. Include details of paragraphs and what to include in them. You can include as much detail/support as you think appropriate.

Title:

Online Support for Writing: Rhetorical Functions

There are an increasing number of online resources available designed to help EMI learners with university-level writing assignments. One of the most popular is UEFAP.com (Using English for Academic Purposes). Another is the Academic Phrasebank produced by Manchester University. Both sites are open access and require no sign-up or membership.

> **Task:**
>
> If you are working with UEFAP.com navigate to the section on Rhetorical Functions.
>
>   (UEFAP.com >Writing>Functions=Rhetorical Functions in Academic Writing)

If you are working with Academic Phrasebank (University of Manchester 2024) go to: http://www.phrasebank.manchester.ac.uk

Spend some time familiarising yourself with the content on the web pages. While you are thinking about them consider these questions:

How useful do you think these pages might be ...
a. for you as a professional academic?
b. for your current learners (undergraduate/postgraduate)?
c. for learners in an EMI context?

Task:

Think about the introductory paragraph/section to a recent written assignment. Create a writing frame specifying rhetorical functions. (Note: You may need to think of rhetorical functions that are not found in the two websites).

Developing Your EMI Writing

Using examples to help develop your writing can be a very effective way of improving your disciplinary writing skills. Ask your lecturers for examples of good assignments so you can learn from them. If you are a postgraduate student, you should find lots of examples of theses and dissertations in the main library or through your university's online platform.

1. **Using an Example Text**
   Look at an example of written work relevant to the type of assignment you have to write. Give special attention to how the assignment realises these key features/elements:

   - macro structure
   - use of evidence
   - referencing a citation
   - written style
   - rhetorical functions
   - etc.

   Make a note of any useful examples. How might you adapt them to assignments you have to write?

2. **Free-Writing**
   It is important that you develop your writing fluency in English! In this timed, no-fault activity, you must write continuously in English without stopping for one or two minutes. When you have finished, try to improve this first version!

3. **Collaborative Re-Drafting Exercise**
   In this task, you work *on each other's drafts*. Exchange your work, then work to improve your classmate's writing. You can work at essay- or paragraph-level. Return improved drafts and discuss. Be nice! Be positive!

First Iteration: No fault Summary Writing

In these no-fault drafts, you are not concerned with mistakes or imperfections. The idea is to just get something on paper – no matter how dissatisfied you might be with your efforts!

1. Translation summaries: Try writing a first draft in your first language, then translating it into English. You can reverse this process by writing in English and then translating it into your first language. By translating, you will probably find ways to improve your first iteration. Write one more improved draft.
2. 30-second written summary: Soon after the lecture has finished, challenge yourself to write a very quick 30-second summary. Do not worry about mistakes or accuracy – the challenge is to just do it! Variation: Work with a classmate who shares your first language. You write a quick 30-second summary in your first language. Give it to your classmate who has to translate it into English!

3. The one-minute paper: Similar to the 20-second summary but a little more challenging! You must write a summary in only one minute but you are not allowed to stop writing – no stops or pauses allowed!
4. Flow diagram mind map: A variation on the classic mindmap or spidergram, this technique focusses on logical relationships between propositions and cause-and-effect relationships. It may not account for the whole content of the lecture but will focus on some very interesting aspects of it.

References

University of Manchester (2024) *Academic Phrasebank*. Available at: http://www.phrasebank.manchester.ac.uk (Accessed: 14 July 2024).